GOOD EYE, BAD EYE

A memoir of trauma and truth

Jeanne Malmgren

Printed in the United States of America
Green Bird Publishing

Cover art: Miblart
Interior stock art: Depositphotos
Author photo: Jim Melvin

ISBN: 979-8-218-57710-0
First edition: September 2024

To reach the author directly:
malmgrenjeanne@gmail.com

Author websites:
goodeyebadeye.substack.com
greenbirdnaturetherapy.com

PRAISE FOR 'GOOD EYE, BAD EYE'

"A fresh, open, and inspiring remembrance."
–Kirkus Reviews (recommended review)

"In her memoir, Jeanne Malmgren fearlessly opens up about her deeply personal physical challenges. Unveiling the truth with honesty and unflinching courage, she shares her journey of resilience, acceptance, and triumph over adversity. This book not only sheds light on her struggles but also offers hope and inspiration to anyone facing their own physical battles. This book is a testament to the strength of the human spirit and the power of vulnerability."

—Venerable H. Gunaratana, author of the bestselling *Mindfulness in Plain English* and many other books on Buddhist practice

"Incredibly powerful and moving. This is a beautifully written book that will help many, many people."

—Janisse Ray, bestselling author of *Ecology of a Cracker Childhood* and *Craft & Current: A Manual for Magical Writing*

"Jeanne Malmgren has spent a lifetime listening to other people's stories, first as a journalist and now as a psychotherapist. In this memoir, she makes sense of her own story, reflecting on a childhood accident that left her blind in one eye. The eye she lost was more than compensated for by the insight she gained: That not knowing the truth only compounds trauma and that discovering it is the first step toward healing."

—Margo Hammond, former book critic of the *Tampa Bay Times* and founder of the Times Festival of Reading

Prior to its print publication, *Good Eye, Bad Eye* was serialized online for paid subscribers. Here are comments from some of those readers:

"This is a book that holds your interest for sure. I could read the whole thing in one sitting." **–Mary L.**

"…tragic and enlightening and beautiful all in one." **–Brie T.**

"Your storytelling is totally absorbing and hits my heart with a powerful punch." **–Laura H.**

"… propulsive and endearing … beautiful on so many levels." **–Allison D.**

"Anyone can see you have sunk heart and soul into this excellent work." **–Mark L.**

"A truly moving true story." **–Martha A.**

"… completely absorbing … vulnerable, brave … There is so much here, so well written and expressed." **–Jenny W.**

"… your journey of challenge and love is beautifully woven into learning the Buddhist practice." **–Kathy C.**

"… such tender beauty … makes me feel compassion for all the kids that struggle." **–Mary D.**

"Riveting …" **–Ross P.**

"What great validation for those of us with similar stories … who have known intuitively that unresolved emotional pain speaks through the body." **–Shelly S.**

"Mesmerizing, fascinating, funny and moving." **–Amanda S.**

" … all of us have felt the deep feelings you lay bare. Thank you for reminding us that we are not alone and that life can be good in spite of the failures and painful circumstances we endure." **–Tricia K.**

"Brilliantly written …" **–Karen D.**

"Every chapter tops the previous ones." **–Linda L.**

"A beautifully written memoir with deep messages that will resonate with anyone experiencing the lingering effects of trauma." **–Jim M.**

"Absolute beauty and peace in the words." **–Chris W.**

For
each of you
—all of us—
walking this long road
from brokenness to beauty

"To see the angel in the malady requires an eye for the invisible, a certain blinding of one eye and an opening of the other to elsewhere."

—James Hillman, archetypal psychologist

Author's Note

I am a psychotherapist.

My business is listening to people's private business, the things they can't tell anyone else—and sometimes can't even admit to themselves. Every day, I hear about my patients' struggles, their deepest fears, their wounds from the past that haunt them still. All too often their stories involve traumatic things that have happened to them.

I listen, and I try to help.

Trauma is a huge buzzword in my line of work. Over the past few decades, it has exploded into a profitable industry. Trauma workshops, trauma books, trauma podcasts, trauma trainings and certifications. This is not surprising. We're recognizing more and more flavors of trauma, spanning a wide spectrum: childhood trauma, developmental trauma, sexual trauma, intergenerational trauma, exposure to violence or war, bullying, natural disasters.

It's a rare person nowadays who hasn't experienced trauma in some form to some degree, and it's a rare mental health clinician who doesn't advertise their services as "trauma-informed care."

Long before I became a therapist, though, long before I understood that bad things rain randomly on people, long before I even knew the word, I made my own acquaintance with trauma. I was 2 years old when it happened. A moment in time, like so many of us have, that is burned in our cellular memory. Something we carry forward, strapped to our backs in a knapsack of pain.

Later in life I stumbled on an ancient set of teachings that would help me understand trauma in a broader sense. I learned about the First Noble Truth of Buddhism, the truth of *dukkha*, or suffering. The Buddha taught that suffering is an unavoidable part of life. Sometimes it's a small dose of dukkha, one of the many minor annoyances we run into daily. Other times it's massive trauma, physical or emotional suffering that pervades our life and throws us completely off course. Either way, we've all tasted it. We've all experienced the First Noble Truth.

During my early years of exploration on the Buddhist path, I spent some time helping run a meditation center. It was impossible not to notice that everyone who came to our center, everyone who was drawn to Buddhist practice, had experienced suffering in some form. I'd see it in their faces, a bone-tired look of sadness. Occasionally, one of them would share their story, their "why" of seeking a spiritual path that offered peace. They already understood the First Noble Truth in a visceral way, and they needed tools for living with that truth.

My first career, before psychotherapy, was journalism. After working a couple of years at a magazine, I moved to a large newspaper in Florida. My job was to find people with interesting lives and coax their stories out of them. Then I'd take my spiral notebook back to the office and hammer out a piece that gave our readers a glimpse into someone else's life. Some of the stories I heard, and wrote about, were entertaining. Some were triumphant. Others were sad, even tragic.

Now I listen to people's stories as a psychotherapist, as someone trying to help them overcome their challenges. It's not an easy job. Trauma can wreak havoc on the human brain and nervous system. I spend my workdays trying to undo that damage and restore people to healthy functioning. So much of it lies in the power of compassionate, empathic witnessing. Sitting with someone as their story spills out. And helping them discover how truth can heal their trauma.

Every one of my patients has a story. We all have stories.

This is mine.

NOTE: *This book contains descriptions of physical injury and trauma. If anything you read here triggers a difficult response in you, please take care of yourself in all the ways you know— including seeing a mental health professional, if necessary. If you don't have a therapist, a great place to look for one is* Psychology Today's *free online "find-a-therapist" service:*
psychologytoday.com

Contents

Prologue   1

You Are My Sunshine   4

Good Eye, Bad Eye   9

Clarence the Cross-eyed Lion   16

Beautiful   28

Eyes That Will Not See   37

Finding the Other   53

The Brain's Smoke Alarm   73

Blindsided   88

An Eye for an I   98

Face to Face   105

Ten Thousand Joys, Ten Thousand Sorrows   119

A Bird Glowing With Light   131

Noble Silence   142

Kintsukuroi   151

Meeting Awareness   158

The Eye of God   166

Search for the Truth   175

Epilogue   189

Acknowledgments   192

About the Author   196

Prologue

It wasn't until seven years after Mother's death that I discovered the truth.

Before then, I thought I knew the truth. Or at least, pieces of the truth I stitched together to make a ragged garment—a cloak that didn't quite fit me, but I wore it anyway. It was all I had. Over the years, I worked hard for those scraps of truth. I probed for details from older relatives who could remember what happened. I wrote letters to the hospital, begging for 50-year-old medical records.

I also ignored the ire of a family member who said I shouldn't go poking around in the past, even though it was *my* past. Our past.

Of course, there were blanks in the narrative. There always are when you're trying to piece history together from multiple sources. When I ran into blanks in my story, I filled them with theories of my own. More scraps stitched into that ill-fitting cloak.

After Mother died and both my parents were gone, it fell to me to empty their house—a mammoth undertaking that took weeks. Mother was a teen during the Great Depression. Those years of scarcity burned into her a deep-seated frugality and attachment to material possessions. Nothing was ever thrown away if it could be re-used in some fashion. She wasn't a hoarder; her house was neat and clean. But every single cabinet, closet, and drawer was packed with the bits and bobs of her life.

Cleaning out her cherry Queen Anne desk was a project in and of itself. The drawers brimmed with dozens of fat manila folders. Mother was a meticulous organizer with a head for details; she had worked as a bookkeeper for the Buffalo Philharmonic. I don't think she ever tossed a single piece of paper if it contained what she deemed to be important information. And in the pre-Internet era, saving paper records wasn't compulsive. It was necessary.

I found checkbook registers dating back to the 1940s, when she started her married life. Handwritten monthly budgets in faded blue ink. A receipt for a 1947 Mercury she and Dad bought, their first-ever new car: $1,979.

After her death, I was too grief-stricken to look at much of it. I stuffed the manila folders in boxes and brought them all to my house. Years later, my closets were still filled with those unopened boxes. I didn't have the heart to delve into them or to throw anything away.

Then one day, during a search for old family photos, I pulled out a few boxes and started pawing through them. Before long I came across a file folder with EYE INJURY written on the tab, in Mother's distinctive all-caps handwriting. Anyone in our family would have known what EYE INJURY meant. Because "The Accident," as it came to be called, didn't happen only to me. It happened to all of us. It was our family's story. And I knew that the story—the rest of the story, its full truth—was in that folder.

For a few moments I sat on the floor with the file in my lap. I was afraid to open it. But I desperately wanted to see what was in there. I *needed* to see what was in there.

An hour later, I had the truth I'd been denied for sixty years. The answers were all there, in a jumble of faded doctor bills, airline ticket stubs, and typewritten letters on crumbling onionskin paper. That file told the story of my parents' frantic efforts to grapple with a tragedy they never could have foreseen, a mistake for which my mother would bear a lifelong load of guilt. I saw my parents' willingness to go the distance, literally, to get help. I saw their love for me, "little Norma Jean." Their desperate holding onto hope.

And then, as hope faded, their ocean of grief.

I saw one other thing in that file: a lie. I saw the falsehood that had robbed me of my core identity, the fictitious story that for my whole life had been presented as the truth. It was a lie spawned out of love, out of two parents' deep desire to protect their child—but a lie, nonetheless.

Chapter 1

You Are My Sunshine

I was sitting in my highchair, the one with dancing animals stenciled on it. My bare feet rested on the little shelf that stuck out below. The wooden tray was locked at my waist.

I was safe.

Mommy was nearby. She was always nearby. And we were often in the kitchen together, as we were that day. It was a chilly Tuesday afternoon in January 1959. I had turned 2 a month ago.

Daddy was at work down the road, in the building with a neon sign out front that said "Jantzen." My favorite part of the sign was the giant diving girl in a tank suit and red swim cap. Every night, when the sign lit up, it looked like she was swimming in midair, like there was a gigantic pool on the roof of the plant. They made bathing suits there, and Daddy was the boss. I'd seen his office. It had a big desk in it.

My brothers were at school. John and Mark. They were named after books in the Bible. If I had been a boy, I would've had a biblical name, too: Luke. Instead, I was Norma Jean, same as Mommy. Sharing a name meant we were closer than close.

John and Mark were a lot older than me, 11 and 10, but that was okay because they were funny and they were nice to me. Except when they tickled me, which I didn't like. If I cried, they got in trouble. And Mommy would make them take me for a walk out on the sidewalk in my stroller.

Life in our red brick house was warmth and love and my Bickie, who was fuzzy and pink, with a Kewpie doll face and a pointy head. All through the night Bickie smiled, sprawled next to me in my crib. If I woke up in the morning before Mommy came to get me, I would stand in my crib and look at the alphabet letters on the wallpaper. I didn't know what those letters meant, but I liked them anyway. I reached out to the wall and traced their shapes with my finger. That became a way to soothe myself whenever I felt anxious, my entire life: I'd trace the shapes of letters—with my fingertip or a pencil or my eye. Words would always be a comfort.

Mommy's back was turned to me, there in the kitchen. She was at the stove cooking supper. She had just finished peeling potatoes, which probably meant mashed potatoes and meat loaf for dinner. We all loved her meat loaf. She put ketchup in it, and little cubes of Sunbeam Bread.

The tray of my highchair was dusted with flour. I was using my miniature rolling pin, the one with the red handles, to flatten a little ball of pastry dough. Whenever Mommy baked, she gave me some of the dough and sprinkled it with sugar so I could roll out a cookie. I wasn't supposed to eat the raw dough but of course I did sometimes, when Mommy wasn't looking. I did lots of things when Mommy wasn't looking. I was so curious.

The kitchen was warm and fragrant. I could smell apples in the oven, bubbling in a golden crust. Mommy hummed a tune I recognized: *You Are My Sunshine*. She knew I liked that song. That song was Mommy.

You are my sunshine, my only sunshine.
You make me happy…

What happened next came squirming out of the tangled, twisted strands of karma—thousands of lifetimes. Lifetimes I couldn't remember, or even suppose. I, or some previous form of "I," must have done something wrong. An act of cruelty, maybe, or simple carelessness. A debt was incurred and now that debt was ripening, like fruit on an ancient vine. Not retribution, not punishment for a sin. Just ripening fruit, and its inevitable fall.

I didn't understand karma, of course. I was only 2. I had no idea how the law of cause and effect would direct the next few moments.

I saw the knife.

It was lying on the counter where Mommy left it, in that vast space of the three feet between us. She had forgotten she put it there after peeling the potatoes. She was untroubled, floating in a sea of peace, the simple pleasure of making dinner for her family.

Turn around, Mommy. Please turn around.

If you turn around now, if you see me stretching my arm out from the highchair, reaching for that knife, everything will be different. Everything. There will be no guilt for you, and no humiliation for me. None of us will have to live the disruption that happens, the unending grief, when one member of a family is forever damaged.

If you turn around now, Mommy, none of what's about to happen will happen. We'll never know.

The knife was in my hand.

I'd never held a knife before. I had some vague idea what it's for. I'd seen Mommy use it when she cooks. But I had no concept of "sharp" or "hurt." Danger had not yet entered the safe cocoon of my life. Mommy and Daddy were good parents, careful parents. They protected me from everything. I was the baby, the precious longed-for daughter. After she gave birth to my big brothers Mommy lost three babies, trying to have a girl. Finally she had one.

I was her great joy. And a minute from now, I would become her great tragedy.

You'll never know, dear, how much I love you.

I looked at Mommy's back. She was standing at the stove, frilly green apron sash tied in a bow around her waist, blond hair twisted into a bun at the nape of her neck. That view of her was the last thing I would ever see with binocular vision. I'd never again know the miracle most of us take for granted, the beautiful symmetry of two eyes merging a pair of slightly different images into one.

The karmic strand had stretched to its limit, as far as it could go. Laden with pain, centuries of tears and regret, the fruit was finally too heavy for the vine to hold. The thread of karma snapped in two.

With perfect aim I plunged the knife into my eye, swift and sure.

Please don't take ... my sunshine away.

Chapter 2

Good Eye, Bad Eye

I was in my brothers' bedroom, lying on the bottom bunk. I couldn't remember how I got there, or why, but I knew my right eye was hurting. I whined as I rotated my fist against the closed eyelid.

Our family doctor was there too, stooping over me in the half-dark room, gently trying to unbend my stiff arm, the one with the fist. I fended him off with all my strength. Mommy stood to the side. I could hear her soft weeping, but I couldn't see her. My eyes were instinctively screwed shut.

The doctor lived only a few blocks away so when my parents called him, he drove right over. That kind of thing could happen in a small town in the southern United States in the 1950s.

My parents were newcomers here, immigrants from the wilds of Oregon. They came to South Carolina a few years before I was born, for Daddy's job. He worked in the textile industry. During the first half of the twentieth century, mills were springing up all over the South. Fields of cotton, cheap labor, abundant rivers for hydropower, and well-established railroad lines—everything the textile companies wanted was here.

My parents' cross-country move was a significant step forward in Daddy's career, but it meant a huge cultural shift for them. When Mommy stepped off the train at the small wooden depot in Seneca and her shoes sank into that gooey red Carolina clay, she broke down in tears. She was so far from home in this alien land.

But the townspeople were kind and welcoming. During my family's first week in our new home, the prominent ladies of Seneca came to visit Mommy, all wearing pastel hats and white gloves. After they left Mommy found their engraved calling cards, one in each chair where they had sat. We weren't natives of the South, but our family was being introduced to its ways—at least, the South of white privilege at the dawn of the Civil Rights Era.

❧❧❧❧❧❧❧❧❧❧

The doctor muttered that it was too dark in the room for him to see my injured eye. When he turned on the overhead light, I howled. It was doubtful this house call would lead to any kind of meaningful conclusion.

No one was exactly sure what happened in the kitchen, but they could piece it together. Mommy sobbed as she told the doctor she didn't see anything. She turned around only when she heard two sounds: my scream and then the knife, clattering onto the linoleum.

The doctor never succeeded in getting a good look at my eye. He told my parents to buy Neomycin ointment and to squeeze some into that eye every couple of hours. He said they needed to get me to an ophthalmologist as soon as possible.

Two days later, we were at the eye doctor's office. He prescribed massive amounts of penicillin, both orally and in a liquid form he squirted into my eye as I writhed in my mother's arms. The eye hurt constantly, and I wished everybody would just leave me alone. Anytime someone leaned in close to examine the eye, my automatic response was to shrink back. And cry.

Already a corneal ulcer had developed. The pupil, according to the doctor, was "bound down" and no longer dilating normally. He said I should be admitted to the hospital so they could examine the depths of the eye. I spent the next few days in a hospital near his office. He came to see me every day. At each visit he was less hopeful about the prognosis. He finally suggested my parents go to a major medical center and get another opinion.

So I had my first airplane ride, to Baltimore, Maryland, sitting on my mother's lap the whole way. Daddy stayed home because of his job and to take care of my brothers. My parents were sparing no expense to get the best medical care they could find. Eleven days after the accident, Mommy and I were in an exam room at the Wilmer Eye Institute of Johns Hopkins Hospital.

The doctor's name was Charles Iliff. He was a renowned eye surgeon. He took one look at my right eye—swollen, red, with a four-millimeter laceration on the cornea—and declared this an emergency. I wouldn't sit still, of course, so he told my mother they'd have to anesthetize me with ether so he could have a good look inside the eye. Dr. Iliff admitted he was unsure whether the vision could be saved.

I was in that hospital for 17 days, receiving 1 million units of penicillin a day to quell the infection raging in my damaged eye. Mommy slept in Room 206 with me. Somewhere she found a soft yellow bathrobe small enough to fit me. Once or twice a day, the nurses let me walk up and down the hall wearing my yellow robe with Bickie in my arms. The rest of the time I was lying on my back in bed with sandbags on either side of my head to hold it still. They were worried about infection spreading from the injured eye to my normal eye—a condition called sympathetic ophthalmia. The only way to prevent that was to immobilize my head. I can't remember what it was like to be an energetic toddler trapped in bed 23 hours a day, but it couldn't have been easy—for me or my mother.

After two weeks, the infection was calmer but a bluish haze was creeping across the surface of my eye. There was no discernible pupil anymore. The brown iris was shrinking. A jagged diagonal line showed where the knife had pierced, all the way back to the retina.

Already my eyelid had begun to droop, like a curtain falling at the end of a play.

Dr. Iliff sat down with my mother and delivered the news. "Visually, this eye is lost," he said. "I'm sorry." It wasn't the outcome any of us wanted, not what we hoped for, not what everybody in our church back home was praying for.

From then on, and for the rest of my life, I would have a "good eye" and a "bad eye."

There's the good eye, which behaves beautifully, drawing no attention to itself, looking just as pretty as anyone else's. Then there's the bad eye, a misbehaving, disfigured mess that turned me into a cyclops. It separated me, permanently, from normalcy.

Eventually Dr. Iliff said we could go home and have our local eye doctor monitor the situation. But he warned that if infection flared again, the eye might have to be removed. They couldn't take the chance of infection spreading to my good eye. If it did, I could end up blind.

Nearly one month after what had come to be called The Accident, we flew back to South Carolina and I started a strange new life.

Half my visual field was gone. The tip of my nose divided the world into two portions: one visible, one invisible. My head rotated constantly to the right, as my left eye struggled to come to center and do the work of two eyes. The overcompensation didn't work, and it messed with my depth perception. My right arm and thigh were purple with bruises from bumping into furniture I couldn't see.

I was glad the sandbags were gone, the pain was over, and doctors were no longer forcing my eyelid open with metal prongs several times a day. But Mommy's shoulders sagged with grief, and I could feel the sadness as it settled over our house. I learned to hang my head, refusing to look directly at people. I didn't want anyone to see my bad eye—the ugliness that lived in me now.

I had one refuge: my library of Little Golden Books. We kept them in a drawer of Mommy's blanket chest in a corner of the living room, next to an oval braided rug. Even though I didn't yet recognize words, I loved sitting on the floor with my picture books scattered around me. Somehow my good eye learned to work all by itself, roaming across a page to take in everything I was seeing. Those Little Golden Books taught me how to be a monocular. I also devoured the hefty Sears & Roebuck catalog with its thousands of colorful pictures—everything from baby dolls to tractors.

I don't think my parents or the doctors ever discussed the idea that I could wear an eye patch, like a pirate. Possibly they thought that would draw attention to my disfigurement. With no patch, though, it was worse. My damaged eye was on display, front and center, every waking moment.

My introduction to the world.

I was flooded with shame and self-loathing, long before I had the words to name those feelings. I was only 2, but already I had come to know the red-hot coals of *dukkha*—the Buddha's First Noble Truth of suffering.

Later in life, I would find a container for this pain. I would come across a spiritual practice that helped me understand why bad things happen. It would gift me with the tools to manage dukkha—my own, and the world's.

But that was still two decades away. Until then, it was me and my bad eye, dancing the dance of trauma together.

Chapter 3

Clarence, the Cross-Eyed Lion

Saturday mornings were movie time in our little town. There was only one theater, perched in the middle of a block on First Street. That was our sole source of entertainment, other than Harper's Five & Dime and the drive-thru window at Bantam Chef, which had ushered us into the amazing era of fast-food hamburgers and fries.

This particular Saturday, Mommy pulled up to the curb in front of the movie theater in our Oldsmobile station wagon. As I climbed out, she handed me two quarters, which would buy my ticket, plus a dime for a bag of Sugar Babies. Most every kid from my third-grade class was there, all of us dropped off by our moms. It wouldn't occur to anyone that this wasn't safe. We knew everybody working at the theater, including the woman at the ticket window and the teenager selling concessions in the lobby.

It was 1965, one year after the Civil Rights Act forced public schools to abide by the Supreme Court's decision in *Brown vs. Board of Education*. At Southside Elementary, all of us children sat together in the classroom. But here at the movies, federal law didn't apply.

We white kids headed automatically for the main auditorium downstairs, while the Black kids climbed the stairs to the balcony. None of us thought to question that seating arrangement. However, the Black kids found a way to even the score. Every so often they leaned over the balcony railing and dropped kernels of popcorn or ice cubes on our heads. No one questioned that, either.

I knew a little bit about desegregation and the kind of animosity it fueled in the Jim Crow South. My daddy, who managed the Jantzen swimsuit factory in town, was the first major employer in the county to hire Blacks. He called a meeting of his 200 employees at the plant and announced that from then on, Blacks and whites would be working side by side—on the sewing floor, in the offices, on the loading dock.

His reward for that was KKK pamphlets, hundreds of them, thrown into our front yard from a car speeding past. I guess we were lucky it wasn't a flaming cross in the middle of the night.

The movie that Saturday was *Clarence the Cross-Eyed Lion*, a Disney comedy about a lion who couldn't hunt because of his vision defect. Eventually he was "adopted" by a veterinarian and his daughter. Portions of the movie were filmed as a double image to show us how Clarence supposedly saw the world. Sometimes the veterinarian's daughter put an oversized pair of eyeglasses on Clarence's face, just to be silly. Clarence, being a thoroughly tame lion, put up with this.

The movie made me uncomfortable, but I couldn't pinpoint why. All I knew was that a lion with crossed eyes didn't seem funny to me. Everybody else was laughing, though. Clarence was such a goofy, good-natured lion.

When the movie ended, we filed outside to wait for our parents. I was standing on the sidewalk near a few other kids when suddenly one of the boys pointed at me.

"Hey!" he said, grinning at his discovery. "You look just like Clarence!"

I didn't know what to say or do. I was frozen. Tears trickled down my face. That's one thing my bad eye could still do: weep. By the time Mommy drove up, four or five kids were dancing in a circle around me, chanting.

"CLARENCE THE CROSS-EYED LION!
CLARENCE THE CROSS-EYED LION!"

From what I can remember, it was only white kids who participated in this ritual. My Black classmates were standing off to the side, watching silently. They understood the sting of ostracism all too well. They also knew what might happen if they got involved in some kind of trouble, even if it was white kids who started it.

Until that day, my parents had done their best to shield me from curious stares, rude questions, and outright bullying. Sometimes I was called "Chinese" or "lazy eye" by other children. But that didn't happen often in our town of 2,000, where everyone knew everyone and the story of my bad eye was common knowledge. Our school had only two third-grade classrooms, and I suspect most of the kids had gotten a lecture from their parents about how they weren't supposed to stare at me or mention my defect.

At home, we never talked about The Accident, or the fact that my eye was blind. It was a taboo subject. I never once heard the word "disability." My family simply showered me with love and tried their best to act like everything was fine. My brothers, by default, fell into the role of protectors of their little sister— especially John, the older one, who's always had a tender heart.

Only everything wasn't fine. And I knew that all too well every time I looked in a mirror. Whatever I thought or felt about the disturbing appearance of my eye became my own private hell.

My memories of what happened that day in the kitchen and my stay in the hospital were already buried too deeply for me to access. And I knew instinctively not to ask questions. So I settled into a primitive understanding of karma. I knew this was my personal cross to bear—silently.

The one hint that something had gone awry with our family's version of the American Dream was the photo album. Daddy's black-and-white Polaroids documented every holiday, every birthday party, every summer trip to visit my grandparents in South Dakota. Mommy glued the pictures on the black construction paper pages of a large leather-bound album. Every photo had a caption and a date, written in white ink she bought especially for the task.

The exception was 1959, the year of my accident. There was not a single photo from 1959 in the album. It was as if that year didn't exist, that my mother wanted to wipe it clean. No photos, no memories. No tragedy. We were experts at ignoring the truth.

School, however, provided regular reminders of my differentness. In first grade, we drew pictures of ourselves during art. Our teacher hung them on the wall of the classroom for parents' night. My crayon self-portrait was a fantasy: two perfect, lovely brown eyes.

As if no one would notice.

One day in second grade I did something wrong, some minor infraction, and I was called to the front of the classroom for a paddling. The teacher, Miss Doyle, had me stand in front of her desk, facing the class, while she got a little balsawood ping-pong paddle from her drawer. I knew it wouldn't hurt that bad. I'd watched other children get this punishment, and they barely flinched. The whole thing was more for show, for embarrassing the offender, than inflicting pain. So I wasn't scared about the paddling. But the horror of standing in front of those rows of kids, facing my peers, all of them staring at me? At my ugly eye? Excruciating.

When school picture day arrived each year, Mommy must have made some kind of advance arrangements. When my turn came, the photographer would change his lights around and rearrange the little wooden stool we sat on, so that I'd be turned sideways when he took my photo. My classmates, waiting in line with me, watched this process with open curiosity while I died a thousand deaths inside. All my elementary school pictures were in profile—only the left side of my face visible, bad eye hidden from view.

As if no one would notice.

In third grade, by some miracle, I got a "boyfriend." He was a sweet boy with a blond buzz cut, son of the preacher at the First Baptist Church. His parents were friends of my parents, so it's highly likely our relationship was engineered. Each afternoon after the final bell at 2:30, he dutifully walked me home across the open field that lay between the school and my house. One fine day, he gave me a necklace: a jade heart dangling from a thin gold chain. I felt almost normal.

Another windfall that year was the arrival of Laddie, a butterball of fur with oversized puppy paws and a teddy bear face accented by a white lightning bolt between his eyes. His soft coat sported every shade of brown imaginable, and I loved him instantly. My stuffed pink Bickie, poor thing, was cast aside in favor of a live companion.

Laddie didn't care what I looked like. He just gazed adoringly into my eyes—one normal, one damaged. Thus began my lifelong love of animals, those masters at sniffing out traumatized people who need unconditional love. In the company of animals, I never worry about the appearance of my eye. Unlike humans, animals don't make a big thing out of differences. Skin color, hair color, gender, age, height, weight, physical flaws. None of it matters. If animals decide you're an ally, they're all in.

Sadly, Laddie didn't live with us for long. His collie curiosity and youthful lack of manners got him into trouble and my parents decided to give him to another family. They told me Laddie would be happier living "in the country" where he'd have plenty of room to roam. For my sake they kept in touch with the new owner, who supplied us with updates on Laddie.

Until the awful day we got word that he had been hit by a car and died. I don't remember how my parents broke the news to me, but I remember the bewilderment and the heartache.

The summer before fourth grade, we moved to Greensboro, a medium-sized city in North Carolina. It was one of several moves we made during my elementary and junior high years. Each time, I had to face another new classroom full of puzzled looks, and the pervading sense—my world view, by then—that everyone thought I looked weird, even if nothing was ever said.

Friends were an impossible dream, mostly due to my shyness. At recess, when we divided into teams for kickball, I was always picked last. The reason for that—my utter lack of athletic skills— never occurred to me. I was sure it happened because of my eye.

By that time my brothers were gone, off to college and their young adult lives. I took my loneliness into the small patch of pine woods behind our house. There I spent hours alone, creating tiny "villages" on the forest floor. Using acorns, pebbles, leaves, and twigs—whatever I could find—I built huts with thatched roofs, swings, ponds, bridges. A perfect world, in miniature. That must have been where my love of nature was born. I sensed how the natural world cradles our sorrow and provides absorption in something outside ourselves.

It was in Greensboro that my sense of being Different, with a capital D, really began to sink in—even if all the adults around me tried to act as though I weren't. Somehow that differentness grew into a streak of rebelliousness. If I was going to be Different, with no choice about it, I would exercise choice in other areas of my life.

One birthday, I got a new bicycle—an aqua blue two-wheeler with a "banana" seat, high-rise handlebars, and a white wicker basket. The freedom I felt, riding my cool bike around our neighborhood all by myself, was exhilarating. The only rule was that

I not ride onto Hobbs Road, the busy throughway that intersected with our street.

Of course, criminal that I was, I rode my bike on Hobbs Road, wild and free. Until one day when my front wheel caught some gravel at the side of the road and down I went, face-first. Mommy wasn't angry, just concerned. She walked me around the house for an hour, not letting me lie down until she was sure I hadn't sustained a concussion. I still have a little ball of scar tissue inside my upper lip.

Another lifelong trait emerged during the Greensboro years. My newfound love for writing resulted in my first published byline, a poem in Scholastic's *Golden Magazine for Boys & Girls*. Writing was something I could do whether or not I had friends and whether or not I looked normal. As the words flowed out of me, I wrote simple rhyming poetry and short stories with predictable plots and stilted dialogue. All my characters, of course, had two perfect eyes. Mommy made sure I had an ample supply of lined notebook paper and, for fun, pens in a rainbow of ink colors.

I started to think of myself as a writer, even though I wasn't totally sure what that meant.

Eventually my parents asked me if I'd like to have an artificial eye. They had been researching and consulting with the Johns Hopkins people by letter. They explained that a special doctor could make a plastic "contact lens" that would fit over my bad eye, and it would be painted to match my good eye.

I asked if it would hurt. They said they weren't sure, but probably not. I thought—but didn't say out loud—that all I wanted was to look like everyone else, the millions of lucky people with two eyes. If this plastic, painted eye could accomplish that, then yes! I wanted it. Very much.

Maybe this would be my ticket back to normalcy. Maybe I'd be able to look in a mirror without hating what I saw. Maybe people wouldn't even realize something was wrong with me. A floret of hope bloomed in my heart.

Soon my mother and I were on a plane to Baltimore again. I was relieved we didn't have to go to the hospital this time. The new doctor's office was in a two-story brownstone, with stone steps leading up to the front door. A friendly, homey-looking place. I wasn't scared.

Mommy explained that this doctor was a lady named Pauline Long. A lady doctor? That sounded good to me. Mommy said Miss Long was an ocularist and all she did all day was make artificial eyes for people like me. Only, Mommy kept calling it a "contact lens." I knew that wasn't right, because contact lenses are for seeing better, not to cover blind eyes. So I just called it my "new eye."

The process of making my new eye took two long days. First there was the plaster mold, which was custom-made to fit the shape of my shrunken blind eye. The ocularist used a mortar and pestle to mix a white paste, then she slathered it directly into my eye as I lay face up on a padded table. The paste was slimy and cold. I was told to lie perfectly still while the mold set. It felt like concrete hardening over my eye.

The next day was my ninth birthday. A Western Union telegram arrived at the Holiday Inn where we were staying:

"Happy birthday Princess. We miss being with you and Mother on this important day in your life. Hope everything is going well. Our prayers and love are with you. John, Mark, and Daddy."

Mommy and I went back to the brownstone, where Miss Long presented me with the unfinished eye, a blank white acrylic shell. It looked a little creepy, like the eyes of monsters in scary movies. But it was the beginning of beauty, or at least I hoped so.

I sat and watched Miss Long paint the shell. That took hours, with me sitting across a table from her, the room flooded with bright lights so she could see the color of the iris in my good eye and try to duplicate it in the new eye. Frowning in concentration, she applied layer after layer of brown tint with a miniature brush, looking up at me every minute or so, then back down to her work. Normally this would have been torture—someone repeatedly staring at me, head-on—but I didn't mind because I knew this nice woman had seen many people with damaged eyes that looked like mine, or worse. She wasn't horrified. It was all in a day's work for her.

The most fascinating part came after the iris had been painted and polished. The shell really looked like a human eye then—I was so excited—but there was one final touch. Miss Long took a length of ordinary red thread from a drawer. It was just like those spools of thread in Mommy's sewing basket. Very carefully, the ocularist separated tiny individual strands from the thread, and laid them on the shell in a random pattern. These would be the thin red veins in the white of my new eye. I didn't even know we have veins in our eyes. I leaned in and watched what she was doing. This would be a beautiful eye.

And it *was* a beautiful eye. It looked almost exactly like my good eye. A masterpiece. The best birthday gift I'd ever gotten. Mommy was pleased, the ocularist was pleased, and I felt a flush of pride that I was about to look normal.

But as we discovered, getting used to a piece of plastic inserted into your eye is no picnic. The shell felt alarmingly huge, like a Frisbee had been shoved into my forehead. When it was in place, my blind eye watered incessantly. Not exactly painful—but not comfortable, either.

Nevertheless, we flew home with me wearing the "contact lens." And feeling like I belonged in the world.

I was ready for my new life.

Chapter 4

Beautiful

We were sitting in church, my parents on either side of me. That's where we were pretty much every Sunday, in the large Presbyterian congregation Mother and Dad had joined. There were lots of people in the pews around us.

The past three years had been the best of my life so far. With the artificial eye in place, I was more confident. Less head-hanging, less avoiding face-to-face encounters. I could go places, see people—and be seen. Attending school and church on Sunday morning was not the exercise in embarrassment it used to be. Life was vastly better than it had been when my bad eye stared out at the world, uncovered. I still cringed in front of cameras, though, because the new eye, this expensive prosthesis, never looked quite perfect in photos.

Somewhere between the Doxology and the Psalm reading that Sunday morning, my prosthesis started to hurt. This wasn't uncommon. I couldn't always tolerate wearing the eye for long periods of time. On a bad day, I might have to take it out for a while, which wasn't a problem when we were at home.

But if an eyelash or a bit of dirt somehow got lodged underneath the shell, that was an emergency of pain and involuntary tears. It was like getting a speck of dust in your eye—multiplied by a thousand. The only remedy was to take out the prosthesis, immediately.

As we stood to sing a hymn, I looked up at my father standing beside me in his gray suit. I was rubbing my eye repeatedly and he knew what that meant. Somehow I got through all four verses of the hymn, with my eye weeping all over my cheek. At the *amen,* we sat and Dad turned to me.

"Take it out," he whispered.

"What?!"

I was mortified. Take it out? Here in church? With all these people around us? He might as well have told me to pee in my pants. This meant I'd have to spend the rest of the hour with my blind eye on display to the world. And then, when we left church at the end of the service and the minister was standing there at the door to shake our hands, he would see my bad eye close up, in all its hideous glory.

Shame flooded me. But I knew Dad was right. This had to be done. Mother looked over at us, realized what was going on, and fished in her purse for a tissue. I bowed my head, swiped my forefinger across the upper lid as the ocularist had taught me, and my beautiful eye landed in my palm. I handed it to Dad. He wrapped the shell tenderly in the tissue, then slipped it into an inner pocket of his jacket.

The pain in my eye was gone; that was a blessing. But now I was naked, and ugly, with no escape. I felt like I was going to cry, but I didn't. I had learned to keep the tears—and the humiliation—locked inside. *Dukkha* was my secret, silent companion.

The summer before I turned 13, we moved to Dallas. It was the year of Woodstock and massive protests against the Vietnam War. When my parents heard that the big-city public school I was zoned to attend was reportedly "full of drugs," they enrolled me in a private academy. It was named after its founder, Ela Hockaday, and billed as a "college preparatory school for girls."

I seized the opportunity—new home, new school—to rebrand myself. Norma Jean, which to me had always sounded like the name of a country music star, morphed into "Jeanie." Much simpler, less attention-grabbing. My perennial urge to be normal and fade into the woodwork.

I started eighth grade wearing the Hockaday uniform of dark green skirt and blazer, white button-down blouse, knee socks and saddle shoes. The school, founded in 1913, emphasized intellectual rigor and hired top-notch teachers, many of them with doctorates.

At Hockaday I discovered how much I loved learning—especially literature and foreign languages, anything to do with words. It wasn't lost on me that reading, writing, and studying were things I could do quite well with only one eye.

Many of the other students came from uber-wealthy families—mostly Texas oil money. One girl's grandfather was the Marcus of luxury department store Neiman-Marcus. Another girl's father was a United States senator. Other last names of my classmates were Horchow and Perot. The boarding students came from prominent families in Mexico, Brazil and Thailand.

The rich girls had been in this school together, a lot of them, since elementary years and they weren't particularly interested in admitting newcomers to their social circle, especially if someone's family was not part of the Dallas elite. My lack of self-confidence certainly didn't help. I managed to make a couple of friends—a Chinese girl, a German girl—and that was enough.

My parents could afford the tuition, but our household income was nowhere near some of my classmates'—the ones who owned horses, spent Christmases skiing at Vail, and got a brand-new Mercedes on their sixteenth birthday. Thank goodness for those uniforms, the great equalizer.

One of my classmates, I noticed, had an artificial eye. It was obvious to me. I imagine she noticed mine too. We monoculars have radar for this. I knew that girl and I were probably patients of the same ocularist in Dallas. But we didn't talk about it. We never talked about it. Best not to focus on how we were different from the other girls. Being different is not a good thing in high school.

Once I discovered the world of fashion magazines and music, that absorbed a lot of my afterschool free time. Alone in my bedroom I would drop a vinyl album on the turntable: James Taylor's *Sweet Baby James* or Elton John's *Tumbleweed Connection*. On Carole King's *Tapestry,* I found an anthem for my teenage angst—her song "Beautiful."

You've got to get up every morning
With a smile on your face
And show the world all the love in your heart.
Then people gonna treat you better.
You're gonna find, yes you will
That you're beautiful ...
You're beautiful ...
You're beautiful ... as you feel.

I wanted to believe her, as I sang along. Then I looked at the album cover. Carole King had two normal eyes, big and blue, the color of a sunlit sky. So, yeah, I thought ... she doesn't know what she's talking about. I could put a smile on my face every morning, but that wouldn't magically give me a pair of flawless blue eyes like hers.

Propped on my elbows on the bed, I pored over photo spreads in *Glamour* and *Seventeen.* The models were so pretty. As I flipped the pages, I fixated on their eyes: huge, limpid pools of perfection, staring at the camera with a confidence I'd never have. I wanted a pair of eyes like that. I would've given anything for a pair of eyes like that.

Twiggy, the super-skinny British model, had rocketed to fame with her adolescent-boy figure, launching a new trend in compulsory thinness for women and girls. I was obsessed with Twiggy, cutting out photos and pasting them in a homemade scrapbook. I loved her ultra-short pixie cut, which made those enormous brown eyes leap from her face.

I knew I was almost as slim as Twiggy. My small waist and flat stomach were points of pride. Each night, I wound my long hair around three empty orange juice cans on top of my head and fastened the whole thing in place with bobby pins. Every girl I knew did that. The result was a smooth, straight waterfall of hair that cascaded down my back.

None of those plusses mattered, though. I couldn't fully enjoy them because I was focused on the one big minus. My bad eye, even masked by its acrylic fakery, would never be a perfect match for the good eye.

One day I picked up a hand mirror and turned my head from side to side while holding the mirror in front of my face. When I looked to the side, I could plainly see how the prosthetic eye didn't track along with the other one. Its range of motion simply wasn't as wide as a normal eye. From that side angle, I looked cross-eyed. The ocularist had done the best he could, but it wasn't enough.

I threw the mirror down in disgust.

When senior year rolled around, I found out just how socially ostracized I was. The winter dance was a formal event, and school tradition said that we girls had to invite someone to be our date, instead of the other way around. Most of us would ask a boy from the nearby all-male secondary school, St. Mark's. I was already nursing a crush on a St. Mark's boy I met during a co-ed biology class in summer school. He was an athlete with a bushy head of hair and the confident attitude of a son of wealthy parents. There was a III at the end of his name.

I swallowed my fear and called him up. Somehow I managed to croak out my invitation: "Would you like to go to winter formal with me?" There was a moment of silence on the other end of the phone. It didn't last long. The boy was a quick thinker.

"Uh, sorry," he said. "We have a basketball game that night."

He knew, and I knew, there was no way St. Mark's would schedule a basketball game on the night of Hockaday's winter formal. St. Mark's was our "brother school." The Hockaday and St. Mark's academic calendars were too linked for that kind of misstep. I also knew, or thought I knew, that he was rejecting me because I had a weird eye. I didn't go to the dance.

Four months later, it was time for senior prom. My mother was determined I wouldn't suffer further rejection—or worse yet, miss out on prom because I didn't have a date. She called a friend of hers. That friend's son was in school at the Air Force Academy in Colorado Springs, not too far from Dallas. Mother bought him a plane ticket for prom weekend. It wasn't exactly a blind date because the boy and I had known each other since childhood. But I was definitely a charity case. Neither the boy nor I had any choice in the matter. At the end of an evening that was at best awkward, he drove us home in my mother's Cutlass and dutifully kissed me at the garage door. I never heard from him again.

After the social debacle of high school, I started to dream. If doctors could transplant hearts and lungs, livers and kidneys, why not eyes? Would it be possible to remove my blind eye and replace it with a new one? Could we simply get rid of this mangled organ that robbed me of normalcy?

I asked my cousin's husband about it. He was an ophthalmologist. His answer was gentle but clear: No. That could never happen. Eyes are complex and fragile, and they're connected to the brain, deep inside our skull. Transplanting one would be too complicated. In fact, impossible.

I found news articles about emerging research in so-called bionic eyes. This breakthrough involved inserting an artificial retina—actually a microchip—at the back of a blind eye, helping the person to see again. But as I read further, I found out that this only works for people who were blinded by retinitis pigmentosa. The rest of the eye must be intact. Mine was not.

So I was left with the inevitable. The unwelcome fact that this would be my truth, for the rest of my life. A trauma that would echo through the years, dragging its cloak of shame along with it.

My situation was a double-edged sword. I was enormously grateful for the technology that provided my artificial eye. That painted plastic shell was the one thing that gave me courage to go out in the world. But it couldn't offer me what I desired most: 100 percent normalcy.

From that point on, my relationship with mirrors was a fractured one. If at all possible, I avoided them. For times when I couldn't, I developed a private magic trick: how to look into a mirror without actually seeing myself. I suspect a lot of people with physical disabilities are experts at this. We gaze at our reflection and somehow manage not to see it. The reality is there but we look past it, through it, beyond. We have to.

Unfortunately, that skill of self-deception—looking but not seeing—was something that would come to dominate my life all too soon.

Chapter 5

Eyes That Will Not See

My first love was a married man twice my age.

When he came along, I was halfway through college and still without a beau. Nothing remotely resembling a relationship. I had a grand total of two dates to my credit—that awkward senior prom night in high school and a cringe-worthy blind date during my first year at an all-women school, Agnes Scott College in Atlanta.

By sending me to single-sex schools that focused on women's academic achievement, my parents gave me the great gift of a stellar education. I will always feel deep gratitude for that. But it also landed me in a romantic desert.

I of course blamed myself, and my disability, for the lack of suitors. I obsessed on the fact that other girls seemed to have no trouble landing boyfriends. During our freshman year at Agnes Scott, my roommate spent hours on the phone each night with her boyfriend, a man she eventually married. She sat on the floor outside our dorm room, phone cord stretched tight under the closed door. I sat on my bed, soaking in envy.

Once she set me up for a date with a fraternity brother of her boyfriend. They were students at Georgia Tech, our brother school. The event was a Halloween party at their frat house on a football Saturday. My date and I talked by phone beforehand and decided on a Wizard of Oz theme for our costumes. I put my hair in pigtails and dressed as Dorothy, carrying a wicker basket with a stuffed toy dog in it. My date was the Tin Man. I think he must have used a dozen rolls of aluminum foil to create his costume. He couldn't walk very well in it, so we spent the evening standing in a corner, watching everyone else get drunk. There was no second date.

That further cemented my already set-in-stone conclusion: The curse of ugliness, of having two mismatched eyes, would forever bar me from true happiness. As illogical and melodramatic as that sounds, it made sense to me. I was approaching my twentieth birthday with virginity intact and not a shred of romantic history— and every time I turned on the radio, I heard songs like *Afternoon Delight* and *Shake Your Booty*. What other evidence did I need?

The older man's attention, when it beamed rather suddenly in my direction, represented the first ray of hope that maybe my luck was changing. It was a whisper in my ear that I might be lovable despite my flaw, that I could possibly have a normal life. The first time he spoke my name, I felt a wild river surge into the dry canyon of my life.

He was darkly handsome and free-spirited, with a teasing smile and a history of making life choices that placed him outside the norm. My primitive, urgent understanding of love, shaped by multiple readings of *Wuthering Heights*, eagerly cast him in the role of my Heathcliff. What I was to him was not so clear, but he took enough reckless chances to be with me that I became convinced our bond was destiny.

He introduced me to alcohol and taught me how to smoke a joint without coughing up my lungs. We went for long drives on curvy mountain roads, the 8-track tape deck in his Honda wafting a soundtrack of Gordon Lightfoot and Roberta Flack. This was the '70s, so there were no cellphones, GPS trackers, or security cameras. It was easy to drop off the radar for an hour, or an afternoon, and no one knew where we were. We created a secret world inhabited by only the two of us—and the thrill of our private universe intoxicated us both.

One summer evening he drove me south across the state line into Georgia, where he rented us a room at a Holiday Inn just off I-85. I was nervous, scared of sex, skittish as a colt. So nothing happened, other than us lying side by side on the bed in our underwear.

Much later, during a weekend beach trip he somehow engineered without his wife becoming suspicious, we finally managed to dispatch the embarrassment of my virginity. For the first time in my life, I felt desirable. It was an unfamiliar and wildly addictive sensation.

When my lover found out I was blind in one eye, he wasn't the slightest bit concerned. He seemed more focused on my innate qualities than my disability. Which, for me, totally eclipsed the inconvenient fact that he belonged to someone else. I wanted so desperately to be loved, I didn't care if what we were doing was wrong. Somehow I willed myself not to think about the peripheral damage, the people who would be hurt by our affair.

I loved him with all the fierceness and purity of a 20-year-old whose world had cracked wide open, a girl tasting joy for the first time. He was a meteor, streaking into my life with his brilliant white light.

By age 23, I had lost him.

Near the end of our three years together, my lover and I grew sloppy about covering our tracks. I suppose some part of me subconsciously wanted us to get caught, to force the point. Living a lie was becoming unbearable.

Eventually, my parents deduced what was happening, based on my mysterious comings and goings from their house. One night I arrived home late—very late—and my mother met me at the top of the stairs. She was in her long nightgown, furious and wide awake.

"Where have you been?" she hissed. "I can smell the marijuana."

It was a classic scene of rebellious child facing off with desperate parent who's trying to hold onto control, a scene that had nothing to do with my eye. Yet it had everything to do with my eye. My parents' long-honed instincts were to protect their wounded daughter from any more hurt. If they couldn't save me from that knife on the kitchen counter, they would save me from all other evils.

I don't remember what I said to Mother that night, but I'm sure it wasn't the truth.

Soon after that, my lover got a Sunday afternoon phone call from my parents. They had guessed his identity. Years later, when I angrily pressed my mother about it, she confessed that she suspected the affair early on. When I first met him, I told her about him and enthused over what a wonderful person he was. Soon after, I stopped talking about him altogether. She said it was my sudden silence that tipped her off, plus my increasingly frequent unexplained absences. So my parents did the 1970s version of sleuthing—looked him up in the phone book and got his home number.

In the phone call, Mother and Dad summoned my lover to an in-person meeting I knew nothing about. At the meeting, they confronted him with their suspicions. He admitted everything, but tried to put a sheen of honor on the circumstances. He told them he loved me, that if we had met when he was younger and single, he would be asking them for my hand in marriage.

My parents were not impressed. In no uncertain terms, they demanded that he leave me alone.

That of course lit a fire under our determination to be together. Plans for our trysts became more elaborate, more desperate. For an entire week I locked myself in my bedroom, feigning grief, to convince my parents the affair was over—and snuck out to meet him when I could. I was now a skilled liar, a criminal who had crossed the line of no return, a former good girl who could never wear that badge again.

Bad girl with a bad eye.

Eventually, my traumatized brain started singing its old refrain: As a defective person, I didn't deserve real love, a legitimate love. All I could expect was this—something in the shadows, something shameful and destined to fail.

Even as my lover and I clung more tightly to each other, our time started to run out. A deception of this degree was ultimately unsustainable. Guilt caught up with us, plus the utter hopelessness of it all. The death knell had been rung. We shared one last wrenching cry together, knowing we had to give up. There was no other option.

He went back to his wife and left me in a chasm of grief, with walls so high I had no idea how to climb out. I scribbled suicidal entries in my journal and dropped out of grad school. I tried a different course of study at a different school. Dropped out again. I couldn't find my footing.

If I wasn't to be with the one person I wanted, I struggled to understand why I should even go on. There was no concept of the long course of a life, and how a person might find happiness at a later date. Nothing meant anything to me, present or future.

That's when my good eye started going bad.

Six months later, I had taken a job as a magazine editor in North Carolina. I was trying to shore up my battered self-esteem and find something to hang onto, a bridge into some kind of future. Home was a three-room log cabin at the end of a rutted dirt road in the mountains. It had a long front porch, a tin roof and a red screen door. My only neighbors were the cows grazing in a pasture on the other side of a metal gate.

I furnished the cabin with thrift-store finds but no TV, by choice. On Saturday evenings, my entertainment was listening to "Prairie Home Companion" on the radio. My roommate was a white cat with one blue eye and one green eye. She lurked on the cabin's porch and brought me occasional love offerings of a dead squirrel.

My parents visited, offered encouragement, tried to give me money. I spurned their overtures. I was mad at them, mad at the world, and most of all mad at karma, which seemed to have a vendetta against me. Even though solitude was exactly the medicine I needed to heal, I couldn't bat away the fear that I might end up being alone for the rest of my life. I sat on the front steps of my cabin with the white cat, smoked weed, and read books about women living solo: *Pilgrim at Tinker Creek* and *Journal of a Solitude*.

Slowly, almost imperceptibly, my seeing eye became more and more sensitive to light.

At first, it was bright sunlight that bothered me. Then it was also cloudy days. I started wearing dark sunglasses anytime I went outside, no matter what the weather was. Eventually, I couldn't bear the overhead fluorescent lights in my office. I sat at my desk, eyes itching and watering incessantly. Looking up or maintaining eye contact with co-workers was painful. At home, I lived in semi-darkness.

Driving in the daytime was a nightmare. Even behind sunglasses, my eyes squinted involuntarily so much that they were barely open. One sunny day, on my way home from the grocery store, I drove my car straight into a row of wooden "Construction Zone" barricades placed across the road. I literally didn't see them.

I was terrified I might be going blind. I called my parents.

Mother drove me to Atlanta to see George Waring, an eminent ophthalmologist and surgeon who had recently arrived to teach at

Emory University Medical School. He was world-renowned in his field as the holder of the first patent for LASIK eye surgery, but he was also a Renaissance man who had a reputation for being compassionate and caring with his patients.

As we sat in the waiting room, I'm sure Mother and I were recalling the last time we visited an eye hospital, twenty years earlier, at Johns Hopkins. Neither of us mentioned it.

Dr. Waring examined my left eye, not saying much. He also wanted to know how my right eye had been blinded. Then he asked me to go into an adjoining room—for another test, he said. We left my mother sitting in the first room.

As the door clicked shut behind us, Dr. Waring told me he could find nothing organically wrong with my sighted eye. No inflammation, no benign growth, no evidence of a cataract, glaucoma or any other eye disease. Nothing to explain this severe photophobia.

"What's going on in your life right now?" he said.

The question took me completely by surprise. I couldn't understand what that had to do with my good eye's intolerance for light. And I didn't know why he wanted to ask me this in private. All I knew was that tears were suddenly rolling down my cheeks.

That seemed to be the answer the doctor was looking for. He said he thought there might be a stress-related component to my symptoms. He suggested that I look into relaxation methods to soothe my nervous system.

So I went searching for more help, this time from non-traditional sources.

The Sufi doctor's office was a double-wide trailer parked in a green mountain valley above Asheville. He had been to medical school, but his skill set also included a variety of non-Western interventions that came from the Sufi system of holistic healing. His working diagnosis agreed with the ophthalmologist's: Something psychoemotional was going on. The doctor hooked me up to a biofeedback machine, so I could practice voluntarily calming my heart rate and respiration. He introduced me to healing herbs for eyes. He suggested meditation and hatha yoga.

The first yoga teacher I found was also an osteopath and a hypnotherapist. It would be his capable hands that guided me to a breakthrough. Born in Ireland, Tim Geoghegan was a bear of a man with an impressive record as a champion boxer, wrestler, and martial artist. After his career in the wrestling ring, he turned to studies of the mind and became interested in Eastern spirituality. He was a follower of the teachings of a twentieth-century mystic named G.I. Gurdjieff.

I went to Tim not knowing exactly how he might help me. But I trusted the friends who told me he had intuitive understanding of how the body and mind interact—still an emerging idea in the early 1980s.

We sat in chairs opposite one another. After coaxing me into a hypnotic state, the Irishman asked an odd opening question: "Is there someone sitting next to you at work, someone on your left side, who makes you uncomfortable?"

What? No.

There were other questions, none of them particularly memorable but all, I think, exploring my emotional landscape. Later, I would have no memory of what I said to him or what clues I might have revealed. But somehow he zeroed in on what was wrong. After talking me back up to full consciousness, Tim delivered a "diagnosis" that was brief, but powerful.

"I think there's something in your life you don't want to look at," he said. "You can't bear to see what's happened—literally."

As I heard those words, my broken heart fluttered. A wave of relief washed over me, salty and sweet at the same time. At last the truth, spoken out loud. After losing my first love, I had successfully forced myself forward into a new life, but my body was lagging behind—literally fighting the light.

And of course this mysterious malady would attack my seeing eye. That's my Achilles heel. It's the part of my body that feels most vulnerable because it's so precious. I'm always afraid to think what would happen if the one window through which I see the world somehow closes. Since childhood, I've had recurrent nightmares about losing the sight in my good eye.

I went home and turned my attention to babying both eyes. It seemed like the only thing left to do. I found a program called the Bates Method of Vision Education. It was billed as a natural, do-it-yourself way to improve visual acuity, but I figured it couldn't hurt to try it on my problem.

One of the exercises in the Bates Method was called "sunning." Ironically, this involved doing the very thing I hadn't been able to do for months. With eyes closed, I stood in the sun, head tilted to the sky and slowly moving my face back and forth. Letting the warmth of the sun penetrate my eyelids. There was also an exercise called "palming," which was placing the cupped palms of my hands over my eyes, and another called "swinging," which involved swiveling the torso from side to side as I stood in the sun, keeping the gaze soft and unfocused.

The exercises seemed absurdly simple, but I practiced them faithfully several times a day. What did I have to lose?

I also dabbled in meditation and fell in love with hatha yoga, even though I had trouble with the balance poses. Standing on one leg was no problem when it involved the left: I felt strong and stable. The right leg, though, was a different story. As I shifted over to balance on that leg, I would wobble like a top. Until then, I hadn't realized how little spatial awareness I have of the right half of my body. With no peripheral vision on that side, it's an invisible, foreign land. A part of me I don't know.

I wrote several articles about yoga for the magazine where I worked, *The Mother Earth News*. One of the articles featured a photo series of me demonstrating the Sun Salutation. I was wearing hippie-yogi clothes—organic cotton in muted colors, soft and baggy.

Inspired by some of the subjects we covered in the magazine, I filled my cabin with the tools of healthy, made-from-scratch eating: mason jars of dried beans, cheesecloth for draining soft cheese, a pressure cooker, a yogurt maker. I grew herbs in the kitchen window. I whipped up batches of homemade granola, and hand-kneaded loaves of bread that were dense with seeds and whole grains. Every so often I fasted for a few days, fueled only by a slurry green drink made with spirulina algae. My early explorations into vegetarianism were maturing into what would become a lifelong interest in plant-based eating.

Slowly but surely, the simple life I'd created for myself in the little cabin at the end of the road started to feel meaningful—almost joyful. It took several months but eventually the photophobia subsided, as slowly and subtly as it began. My eyes healed. My heart healed.

Was it the Bates exercises or a placebo effect? Maybe it was the yoga and meditation, and how those practices helped me calm my nervous system? The earthy diet? Or was it simply time, the great healer of grief? The answer wasn't obvious, so I didn't belabor it. I just moved forward, propelled by a dawning sense of gratitude. I was happy to be alive and whole.

Decades later, while working on my master's degree, I opened a textbook one day in psychopathology class and read the words "conversion disorder." It was a thunderclap of truth. The last puzzle piece fell into place.

Conversion disorder is a diagnosable psychiatric malady. Although rare, it is well documented in the medical literature. A person suffering from conversion disorder experiences uncontrollable physical symptoms that seem to have no biological cause. The symptoms can be neurological, causing problems with movement, or they might affect one of the senses—most commonly hearing or vision.

Vision. Yes.

What causes this bizarre condition? That's a mystery, but typically patients with conversion disorder have suffered some kind of emotional or psychological trauma before the onset of their symptoms. If ever there were an argument in favor of the mind-body connection, this is it.

I read the description in my textbook and felt vindicated beyond words. It all made sense, finally. The end of that love affair was simply too agonizing to bear, so my brain "converted" the psychological pain into a physical symptom.

Eagerly, I sought out other examples of conversion disorder in which the physical symptom was ocular. It usually happens after the person has seen something overwhelmingly painful. Psychogenic vision loss, it's called.

In the 1940s, soul musician Ray Charles watched his younger brother drown in a laundry tub when Ray was 5 and the brother was 4. Ray was helpless to save him. Soon after that, his eyesight started to dim. By the age of 7, young Ray was completely blind. His right eye had to be removed because of intense pain. Was it glaucoma, a disease that would have taken his sight anyway? Or was it an example of conversion disorder—something that in less enlightened times was called "hysterical blindness"? Medical experts still debate it. Ray never had an official diagnosis, so we can't be sure.

Then there are the haunting tales of female Cambodian refugees who went spontaneously blind after witnessing gruesome deaths in the Killing Fields genocide of the late 1970s. The singular cruelty of the Khmer Rouge soldiers was to force women to watch their loved ones' murders. Babies killed by being bashed against trees. Husbands and elderly parents shot or disemboweled, then dumped into mass graves. Unimaginable horrors.

Once the refugees made it to America and settled in California, many of them were treated for unexplained vision loss. No physiological problems with their eyes could be found, yet they were "functionally blind," according to the researchers who studied them.

"These women saw things that their minds just could not accept," one researcher told the *Los Angeles Times* in a 1989 article.

At 23, my heart shattered and my one eye unwilling to face reality, I didn't yet fully understand how the mind and body are entwined. I had no idea how trauma can ripple through the whole system like a seismic wave. But I had lived it. I had experienced my own version of that truth.

The eyes cannot see without a mind able to look.

Chapter 6

Finding the Other

After the devastation of that early loss, I somehow moved on. My heart was battered and bruised, a prizefighter sagging against the ropes. But having sampled a teaspoon of love, with its rich flavors, I longed for more.

The human impulse to pair off, to find a life partner, is deeply embedded in us. Even after heartbreak we press on against all odds, in search of the person who will be by our side. We're a species that seems to need an "other."

Though there is a growing number of single people in the world, especially in developed countries, and though there's no doubt a single life can be richly fulfilling, the majority of us still seek relationship. I see it every day in my psychotherapy patients, the ever-hopeful search for that elusive other, the willingness to put ourselves through all manner of emotional gymnastics as we pursue the goal. Every aspect of our culture—movies, literature, art, music—celebrates the search for true love.

For many people with disabilities, that search is even more intense. I cannot speak for everyone who lives with a disability, but I think I can say this with some confidence: We crave not only love, but also confirmation that our defect doesn't disqualify us from this most basic human need. We long for a partner who will love us enough to prove our worthiness. I certainly did.

During my twenties, after that first affair ended, I had a few boyfriends, off and on. Some were not much more than sexual partners with whom I was medicating my heartache and self-doubt. Others were more serious relationships, though temporary.

With each one, I faced the wrenching decision of whether to tell him about my blind eye … and when. I never knew if that news would be a deal-breaker. It didn't seem to be. At least none of them said so. But the fact that none of them stuck around seemed to confirm my theory: A one-eyed person will have to try harder to find a partner who can accept their fundamental brokenness. We are not as deserving of love, I figured, so we'll need patience and persistence in the search. And we have to make our peace with the possibility that love might never happen.

One of my suitors told me that after he learned about my disability, he walked around his house with a hand cupped over one eye. He even tried it for a minute while driving. "I wanted to see what it's like for you," he said.

His empathy floored me. The fact that someone was curious about my lived experience was a revelation. It wasn't enough, though, to dislodge me from my stubborn attachment to the theory of *ugly-thus-unloved*. When trauma wraps its tentacles around the gray matter in your brain, it doesn't easily let go.

⁓⁓⁓⁓⁓⁓⁓⁓⁓

Sometime during that period, I came across a gorgeous essay by Alice Walker, author of *The Color Purple*. Like me, Walker lost the sight in one eye in a childhood accident. I admired her writing but I had no idea we were fellow monoculars until I read her essay. It's titled "Beauty: When the Other Dancer is The Self."

Walker wrote in that essay about many of the same things I experienced: the shock, the shame, the reluctance to raise her head, bullying by other kids. And most of all, the incessant, fruitless yearning to look normal. At age 12, four years after her accident, Walker raged in front of the mirror: "I do not pray for sight. I pray for beauty."

Ohhhh, how I understood that.

Whenever I walked side by side with a boyfriend, I engineered it so he would be stationed on my left. I claimed it helped me see him better, using the peripheral vision in my left eye. But truthfully, it was because I considered that side to be my "good" side, in terms of beauty.

Good eye, good side.

The need to be positioned correctly as we walked was so deeply ingrained in me that it became a reflex. If my partner placed himself to my right—bad eye! bad side!—I simply dropped behind him without a word and moved to the other side. Most of them got used to it after a few times. "Oops, sorry," they'd say.

The thornier problem was when we went to bed.

I don't wear the scleral shell at night. My blind eye needs to rest, and breathe, without a piece of plastic covering it. Moments before bedtime I take it out, clean it with contact lens solution and store it in water inside a small round container on the bathroom counter. Which means that right before the lights go out, as I climb into bed, I'm unmasked. My true identity is revealed: a person with an ugly, disfigured eye. It's a moment of vulnerability that for me is more uncomfortable than full-body nudity.

So much for enthusiastic sex before sleep. Even though it's dark, he might somehow see my eye.

And so much for a romantic good-morning kiss when the alarm goes off. As soon as our eyes open, I'm sprinting for the bathroom. I have to get that prosthesis back in before my partner fully wakes up.

The man who became my first husband lived in Florida, and I was in North Carolina. His mother, a neighbor up the road from my log cabin, told me about her son who was a few years older than me, already in his early thirties. He was a vegetarian like me, so she thought we might hit it off. She gave me his address.

He and I got to know each other via U.S. Mail. No phone calls, no photos. Just handwritten letters mailed back and forth for months. We discovered we had a lot of common interests: nature, organic gardening, animals, yoga, meditation. After I confessed my secret to him in one of my letters, he revealed his. As a child, he nearly lost his leg in an accident when he was hit by a drunk driver. The doctors weren't sure if he'd ever walk normally again. He did, but his leg was forever branded with a network of scars and the mottled texture of skin grafts.

Almost thirty years after that accident, he explained in his letter to me that the injured leg was permanently shorter than his other one, but it didn't slow him down. In fact, he made his living as a landscaper, mowing lawns and trimming trees. His free time was spent hiking and canoeing. He sounded doggedly, determinedly active.

When I read his words, I knew we'd be together. Two scarred people who had learned to live with disfigurement. The pair of us, helping each other move beyond a childhood trauma that divided our lives between the moment before the accident, and all the moments after.

"Our union will be a blessed one," he wrote to me.

When I announced to my parents that I was quitting my terrific job at the magazine and moving to Florida to live with a man I barely

knew, they came in person—an hour's drive—to try to dissuade me.
I was adamant. This was my big chance at love, and I wasn't about
to let it slip through my fingers.

As they left, there was an ugly scene on the porch of my cabin,
Mother sobbing and collapsing into Dad's arms. As they stumbled
toward their car, entwined together in sorrow, Dad delivered a
parting shot over his shoulder.

"You're breaking your mother's heart!"

I watched them drive away. We didn't wave goodbye.

My new home was a modest Florida bungalow painted mint
green with towering royal palms in the front yard. Behind the house
was an extensive vegetable garden, a row of beehives, and a compost
heap the size of an outhouse, barely contained by chicken wire. The
house had no air conditioning, only ceiling fans and windows that
stayed open year-round. My two cats, who made the journey with
me, joined my boyfriend's pack of two cats and three dogs. We
formed a family.

He belonged to a group studying the branch of Hinduism called
Vedanta, which emphasizes the effort to realize one's divine nature
through devotional practice. The extra bedroom in his house was set
up as a meditation room, with a wooden coffee table serving as an

altar. Anchoring each end of the altar were framed photos of Indian mystic Sri Ramakrishna and his wife Sarada Devi, each swathed in white robes.

I'd already been scouting around in my own search for a spiritual path, inspired by the healing practices I tried during my bout with photophobia. Vedanta interested me, but I couldn't quite latch onto its teachings. I did however love the ritual of lighting a candle and putting long sticks of incense in a bowl of sand, then sitting on the floor in front of the altar for a period of silent contemplation as the scent of burning sandalwood swirled around me.

Six months after my arrival, we decided to wed. It was my first summer living in the subtropics. Without air conditioning, I found Florida's intense heat and humidity to be insufferable. I told my boyfriend I missed the mountains, that I wanted to move back home. His response was immediate: He got down on one knee, right there in the kitchen, and begged me to stay.

"Let's get married," he said.

Once that decision was made, the next question was who might perform the ceremony. We wanted something spiritual, so a trip to the courthouse seemed flat. Since both of us had wandered away from our religious upbringings, a Christian pastor wasn't a good fit, either.

I found a notice in the religion section of the local newspaper. It said a renowned Buddhist monk was coming to town to give some lectures and lead meditation sessions. We knew next to nothing about Buddhism. We called the people organizing his visit. Sure, they said, the monk can come to your house and conduct a marriage ceremony.

I was elated. This sounded like exactly the kind of offbeat, my-parents-will-hate-this wedding I wanted. I found a royal blue, embroidered dress at the gift shop in Busch Gardens. The bridegroom, who was notoriously thrifty, actually bought a new shirt, a long-sleeved dashiki, to go with his favorite drawstring yoga pants.

The monk turned out to be a 96-year-old Cambodian who lived at a Buddhist temple in California. He was small and stooped, bald, wrapped in burnt orange robes. His hosts helped him up our front steps. We didn't know any of them. They slipped off their shoes and left them just outside the door.

In the meditation room, we knelt and the monk sat cross-legged in front of the altar. In a surprisingly robust voice, he chanted words I couldn't understand. I didn't know then, but later came to believe it was probably the Metta Sutta, a chant of blessing and lovingkindness. The language is Pali, an ancient Indian dialect akin to Sanskrit. Pali was the language spoken by the Buddha.

There are thousands of *suttas*, or discourses, in the Pali Canon. This one is commonly chanted on occasions when benevolent wishes are in order. The words in English are simple, uplifting.

Let no one deceive another,
Nor despise anyone anywhere.
Neither from anger nor ill will
Should anyone wish harm to another.

As a mother would risk her own life
To protect her only child,
Even so towards all living beings,
One should cultivate a boundless heart.

One should cultivate for all the world
A heart of boundless lovingkindness,
Above, below, and all around,
Unobstructed, without hate or resentment.

Much later I learned that Buddhist monks aren't supposed to perform weddings. So I think the old Cambodian was simply blessing our union, not creating it. Which means that the ceremony probably wasn't legal. And that his signature on our marriage certificate wasn't the signature of someone authorized to marry us in the state of Florida. Oh, well ...

After the chanting, the monk's followers tossed rose petals over our heads and the five-minute ritual was over. Then we all sat in the living room and drank green tea. This was my introduction to

Buddhism, an ancient path which suddenly had veered into my life. And here, my first tentative step onto that road.

Even later, I learned what an eminent monk had blessed our marriage. Venerable Dharmawara advised King Norodom Sihanouk of Cambodia and presided over the deathbed of Prime Minister Jawaharlal Nehru of India. When Dharmawara died at the age of 110, almost 15 years after our wedding, his obituary appeared in the *New York Times*.

For our honeymoon, my new husband and I backpacked a section of the Appalachian Trail in the Great Smoky Mountains—he with a mangled leg, me with a blind eye. That would be the first of our many outdoor adventures together. He found me attractive. I found him attractive. We had resolved that issue, at least. Our marriage confirmed that people like us have the right to love and be loved.

A few months later, my parents insisted on a Christian wedding. Neither I nor my new husband were keen on the idea, but we went along with it. His parents showed up at my parents' house and we all stood in front of the fireplace. Mother had decorated the living room with fresh flowers. A Presbyterian minister did the honors, holding a black leatherbound Bible in his hands.

To my surprise, I felt relief. Somehow, at least for an afternoon, we bridged the widening spiritual gulf between my parents and me. I knew they had been worried, but at least my marriage was now duly consecrated. Or should I say, doubly consecrated.

Within a few months, my husband and I joined a Buddhist group that met weekly for meditation and chanting. It felt like an increasingly solid road, one I might walk for the rest of my life.

Then we moved to a house with shady one-acre grounds and a huge double garage—quite a real estate find in Florida's most densely populated county, where houses crowd together on pencil-thin lots. The house was surprisingly affordable, probably because it was thirty years old and smelled of mildew. It had 1950s-style jalousie windows and yellowing terrazzo floors.

"Let's turn this place into a meditation center," my husband said. He was enterprising, and not afraid of a challenge.

We started to dream about hosting weekend retreats where people could come for spiritual practice and *sangha*, or community. He worked hard to renovate the garage. One side would be a small, spartan apartment where visiting monks and teachers could stay overnight.

The other half of the building became the meditation hall, with soft green grasscloth wallpaper and Japanese-style lanterns flanking a simple wooden altar. We covered the concrete floor with tatami mats and bought a dozen zabutons, large square cushions, for meditators to sit on.

We even found a sapling of the sacred Bodhi tree, *Ficus religiosa,* to plant on the grounds. Florida's hot, humid climate was ideal for this tropical species. Sometimes known as a "Bo" tree, this was a descendent of the great spreading tree under which Siddhartha Gautama sat in meditation on the night of his enlightenment, when he transformed from an Indian prince into "The Awakened One," the Buddha. All Bodhi trees anywhere in the world are revered by Buddhists as living reminders of the Buddha's spiritual achievement.

Next to our young *Ficus religiosa,* my husband erected a flagpole. With great ceremony, our first visiting teacher, a Sri Lankan Buddhist monk, raised the multicolored Buddhist flag at our opening retreat.

Bodhi Tree Dhamma Center was born.

(*Dhamma* is the Pali equivalent of the more familiar Sanskrit word *dharma*, meaning "the truth" or "teaching.")

We started inviting teachers from various Buddhist traditions to visit our center. In those early days, we hosted a Tibetan Rinpoche with a sonorous voice, a rotund Zen Roshi, and quite a few teachers of Vipassana meditation, in the Theravada tradition. It was the mid-

1980s, meditation was still an emerging concept in the United States, and there weren't many Buddhist centers on the east coast. So it was easy to persuade teachers who would later become famous to visit our small, humble center.

For longer retreats of ten days, we rented rural conference centers that could accommodate as many as twenty-five people. With our bulk mail permit, we sent out hundreds of flyers and registered those who signed up. It was a cumbersome process, equipped with only a typewriter, stapler, and Scotch tape.

At those rural retreats, I was housekeeper and chief cook—in other words, the *only* cook. Each morning I rose at 4:30 so I could have a hot breakfast ready for the meditators after their 5 a.m. sitting. As soon as that meal was cleaned up, I started chopping vegetables for lunch, which was the main meal of the day. My vegetarian cookbooks were soon pockmarked with penciled notes about quadrupling the ingredients, so I could feed that many people.

At the end of ten days, the meditators headed home in various states of bliss. My husband and I? We were exhausted. But I learned firsthand about the power of service. I had come from a privileged middle-class background and never had a paying job until halfway through college. I didn't really know what physical labor felt like. Those retreats offered me an invaluable lesson in humility and hard work as I scrubbed toilets, emptied trash cans, sweated over an industrial stove, and chopped onions at 6:30 in the morning.

Not all spiritual progress is made on the meditation cushion, I learned. It's also in how we engage with others, how we help, what we offer to the world. One of the core Buddhist practices is *dana*, pronounced DAH-nuh. Usually translated to mean "gift" or "donation," dana is the practice of loosening our attachments and greed. By giving, in any form, we reap the spiritual fruit of generosity.

Because my husband and I as the retreat organizers got to know the teachers personally, I had one-on-one access to them after the group meetings. One in particular, the German teacher Ruth Denison, rewarded my efforts richly. Each night she kept me up late, filling my mind and heart with precious teachings. I was always worn out while working those retreats, but Ruth encouraged me—challenged me—to keep meditating even after my tasks for the day were done.

"You must *surrennnnder* to this practice, dah-ling," she would say, her melodic Prussian voice lingering over the word "surrender."

Ruth was a small, intense woman, a drill sergeant in a maxi skirt and diamond-studded glasses hanging on a chain around her neck. Through a relentless combination of compassion and fierceness, she was known for pushing students toward breakthroughs. Her signature teaching was the art of embodied mindfulness.

On retreat, she would herd everyone outside and lead a group exercise in movement—raising one arm with exquisite slowness, or shifting body weight rhythmically from side to side. Within a few minutes, everyone would be dancing free-form to hypnotic drumming that poured out of Ruth's cassette player. And then she would slow us back down for the silent, measured practice of walking meditation.

When it came to *anapanasati*, mindfulness of breathing, Ruth was a taskmaster. She wanted us to stay in contact with our breath all the time, every waking moment, no matter what we might be doing.

"Try to be aware of your very last breath before falling asleep at night," she said. "Is it an in-breath or an out-breath? And then try to be aware of your first breath as you wake up in the morning. Is it an in-breath or an out-breath?"

To this day I'm still working toward that goal.

⚬⚬⚬⚬⚬⚬⚬⚬⚬⚬

Sadly, all the exposure to wise teachers and our dedication to a shared spiritual life was not enough to keep my husband and me together. Neither of us had finished the work of healing our early wounds. In retrospect, his adamant refusal to consider having children was wise. I just couldn't make my peace with it. The day we went to a vasectomy clinic, at his insistence, and I sat bereft in the waiting room while he had his procedure done, was the day my heart started to harden.

Six years into the marriage, I moved out. At that point, we were long into our tenure as the hosts of Bodhi Tree Dhamma Center. It was emotionally wrenching for me to disengage from the community we had built. This wasn't only the place where I lived. It was also my spiritual home.

My husband was not at all happy I had decided to leave. In our divorce settlement, he agreed to pay alimony for two years and I gave him the meditation center—the house, the big garage, and the one-acre grounds where we did all that peaceful walking meditation. It seemed like the right thing to do.

Then followed another period of solo living. A one-bedroom duplex apartment at the beach. More boyfriends, more short-lived romances. And fresh fear that I'd be alone permanently, that no one else would ever want to partner with someone who's half-blind. Despite a steady stream of men who were interested in me, at least temporarily, it wasn't enough to fill the deep well of unworthiness. It couldn't quiet the drumbeat of that voice inside me, insisting I was unlovely—and thus unlovable.

Husband No. 2, when he came along, was a gentle man, a colleague at the newspaper where we both worked. He was the father of two young girls, and his marriage was in the process of ending. He had a humility about him that I found fresh and appealing. He also had a boyish sense of humor, with a wild laugh described by one of our friends as "the squawk of a tropical bird in the rainforest."

This man's approach to life was that it's important to try to be happy, and to be kind to others. His only neurosis was a dogged loyalty to the Tampa Bay Buccaneers, who at that point were the lousiest team in the NFL. He had grown up in Florida, with the sun-bleached blond hair to prove it. In all respects … an anti-Heathcliff.

To my surprise, Jim seemed to find me quite acceptable. If "two perfect eyes" was on his list of must-haves in a partner, he didn't complain. He simply pursued me with a quiet, determined passion. He quickly figured out the walk-on-her-left-side ritual, and never forgot it.

Jim's calm, grounded demeanor was the perfect foil for my restless spirit. He taught me the art of sitting in beach chairs at the water's edge, sipping wine and soaking up the sunset. We bought a pair of sea kayaks so we could explore barrier islands and paddle through mangrove tunnels. In this man's company, I learned how to be uncomplicated, how to relax and enjoy what a moment brings.

One evening he unfolded our chairs on the sand of Pass-a-Grille Beach as streaks of pink and gold lit the sky over the Gulf of Mexico. The sun was gone and so were the beach walkers. We were alone.

Jim pulled a ring from the pocket of his shorts.

"I want you to marry me," he said.

There was something about the way he made his proposal—as a declarative statement, not a question—that won me over.

I already knew my answer, anyway.

A few days later, I told Jim there was something I needed him to see. We sat on the end of the bed in his apartment. My hands were shaking. I popped the prosthesis out of my blind eye and turned to face him, straight on. For the first time in my life, I was voluntarily showing someone my true self.

I hated to uncover this ugliness. I hated that I couldn't be perfect for him. But I had to reveal my reality before we went any further. I didn't want this relationship to be like all the others, where I hid behind the disguise of a painted plastic eye. I wanted this man to be the one—the only one—who would see the truth of me.

Jim looked into my shrunken eye, concern written all over his face.

I was so flooded with fear and apprehension, I would not remember later what he said. But he's a plainspoken, kind man. It was probably something simple, something like, "Okay. That's not so bad."

We married on a yacht-for-hire cruising through Tampa Bay. An unseasonably cold winter wind buffeted the boat. (Why, oh why did we schedule our wedding for mid-January?

We were both in our late thirties, with one failed marriage apiece. But it was a day of hope, surrounded by family and friends.

My attendants were Jim's daughters, wearing little Laura Ashley dresses and flower crowns in their blond hair.

By this point I was a full-fledged Buddhist, so our vows included a line about committing to our partnership not just in this life, but also through however many other lives we will have together. It did feel as if we knew each other before, that we'd found our way back together.

Maybe in the next life I will have two lovely eyes for him to look into.

Our formal wedding photo shows the two of us smiling shyly. He wears a rented tux with a blue flower pinned to his lapel. I had found a $300 dress at the mall. We look achingly young.

Every time I see the picture, I'm struck by the same surprising thing, something that hardly ever happens in photos of me. By some stroke of luck, some just-right tilt of my head at the moment the photographer clicked the shutter, my eyes look almost … normal.

Part of it, I think, was the joy of that day, floating me along on cloud nine. When it was time to pose for photos, I looked straight into the camera, something I've hated doing my entire life. I was too happy to care.

Lo and behold, my eyes look fine in the picture, even though they're not perfectly balanced. I can tell the difference—because I'm always looking for it. But to the casual observer, someone who's simply admiring a photo of a couple on their wedding day, I know the difference is barely noticeable. It's not important.

For the most part, the bride's eyes are a matched pair ... just like the two of us.

As I would find out, though, trauma has a sneaky way of popping back into someone's life, even after what seems like the happy ending.

Chapter 7

The Brain's Smoke Alarm

I was sitting in the fourth row of a movie theater deep inside Disney World. My husband was on one side of me, his daughters on my other side. The overly air-conditioned air was freezing. But we were relieved to be out of the heat, away from the crowds and the long lines. We'd been on the go since 8 that morning. It was heavenly to have a chance to sit down and let the sweat dry.

The girls giggled about their cardboard 3D glasses, putting them on and making funny faces at each other. One was 11, the other 7. They were excited because they liked Michael Jackson and the movie short we were about to see starred him as "Captain EO." It was some kind of science fiction music video with 4D special effects: 3D plus enhanced sound and smells. The technology was still pretty new. None of us had ever experienced it. We didn't know what to expect.

I put on my glasses. One cellophane lens was red, the other blue. I smiled at my husband. He smiled back. We'd only been married six months, and I was still getting used to the role of stepmother.

Even though I'm not a fan of theme parks, the day was going well so far. I just might be able to do this, I who had zero experience with parenting.

As the lights went down, Jim squeezed my hand. I knew he was happy to have everyone he loved— me, his daughters—together. This is how he wanted it. And finally we had it.

The movie started. Michael Jackson was the commander of a spaceship flying on a mission toward an asteroid. His crew, a band of shaggy animatronic animals, managed to screw things up hilariously. There were frequent near-misses as they hurtled through space.

Within seconds, everyone around me in the theater—my husband, my stepdaughters, everyone sitting behind us, in front of us, on both sides of us—was screaming, laughing, cringing backwards. Some people threw their hands up in front of their faces or reached overhead, as if they were trying to grab something out of the air.

I was confused. What was going on? Obviously they were seeing something I wasn't. Were my glasses defective? I took them off, put them back on. I still saw … a movie. In fact, a blurry movie. As if I had double vision.

It took me a minute or two to figure out the problem.

To fully experience a 3D movie, you need two eyes. If you don't have two eyes, you're looking at a flat visual image up there on the screen, actually two images overlaying one another. The cardboard glasses on your face don't help at all.

Shafts of light started pinging off the walls of the theater. Bursts of smoke floated over our heads. The sound effects were loud, intense. At least I could experience those things. But whenever people around me laughed and lurched backward, I didn't know what to do. Fake like I can see what they see? Flinch when they flinched? Try to feign normal?

I was chagrined, and deeply embarrassed. It felt silly to fake it, so I sat motionless while everyone else bounced around in their seats like Mexican jumping beans.

"Can't you see it?" Jim was looking over at me, whispering. Worried, loving.

I didn't know what to say. I didn't even know what it was that I couldn't see. How did I not know this before? Why couldn't I have predicted this? For one thing, I'd never been to a 3D movie. I hadn't spent a lot of time thinking about how they work, what makes them so realistic.

For another thing, I often forget that I'm half-blind.

I can see the world, I can navigate. I drive a car. I push lawn mowers and mince carrots. I used to play racquetball and badminton, sports where I had to hit a flying object with some degree of accuracy. In college, I solo-sailed a little 10-foot Sunfish. I have relished the sight of full moons, rainbows, meteor showers. All of that with only one eye.

Human bodies are equipped with several pairs of things. We have two eyes, two ears, two legs, two feet, two arms, two hands, two kidneys, two lungs. Each pair is designed to work in tandem. But we can lose one of the pair and still function, though somewhat at a disadvantage.

Losing an eye, I suppose, is maybe one of the "easier" disabilities to endure. One eye can compensate and do the work of two. So I'm grateful that I lost an eye, not an arm or a leg or a hand. With my one functioning eye, I can straddle the line between deformity and normalcy. Most of the time.

Eighteen minutes later, *Captain EO* ended and we were back out in the merciless Florida sunshine. My sense of alienation was over. We went on with our day. Only, that feeling of being different, of not being able to see what everyone else sees, was *not* over. It ambushes me when I least expect it.

For weeks, months, sometimes years, I can live the pretense that I'm normal. That nothing about me is visibly, or experientially, different. Then something happens, usually something I couldn't have foreseen. (I know … a bad pun.)

Often it's something much less dramatic than a 3D movie. A simple, careless remark, for example. Someone utters the word "eyeball"—a perfectly innocent term, even if it is anatomically inaccurate—and I blanch. It literally sends a shiver down my spine. To me, the word "eyeball" describes an eye that has fallen out of its socket. An eye like mine that isn't normal anymore. An eye that is rolling across a table, untethered and slimy.

And then there are those hard balls of chewing gum painted to look like an eye. They're popular Halloween treats. Once when I was trick-or-treating with friends, we rang a doorbell and the homeowner presented us with a huge bowl full of gum eyeballs. The other kids scooped up all they could, with whoops of laughter. Not so funny for me.

Also, I know that everyone else's concept of "eyeball" is a nicely rounded globe. Not mine. As years pass, my blind eye shrinks more and more. It's as if it knows it's no longer needed or functional, collapsing on itself. Sixty-five years after doctors worked so heroically to "save" that eye, it's now a shriveled version of its former self.

This is common in eyes blinded by injury or disease. It's a condition called *phthisis bulbi*. The first time I read that on my chart at the ophthalmologist's office and Googled it to see what it meant, I was overcome with sadness. I have what is called an "end-stage eye."

Every time I go to an ocularist to have a new prosthesis made, they have to shape the lens with more bulk, more surface area than last time. That's necessary to cover the continually withering former eye that lives in my head. Sometimes I wish the doctors had simply removed it when I was 2. Then I wouldn't have to witness this slow, sad disintegration.

Another nausea-inducing moment is when someone says, "I'd like to gouge my eyes out." I know they don't mean it literally. It's a figure of speech that somehow, ineptly, has come to express frustration. But those words make my stomach lurch. Suddenly I'm two years old again, sitting in a highchair, reaching for a knife on the kitchen counter.

In ninth grade English class, we read *The Odyssey*. I loved its sweep of adventure and the ornate Homeric language. But when it came to Polyphemus, the giant ogre who imprisoned Odysseus and his men in a cave, I felt twinges of discomfort, reading that Polyphemus was a cyclops with only one eye in the middle of his forehead. Then it got worse—the scene where Odysseus seized a burning wooden stake out of the fire and plunged it into Polyphemus' eye. I could barely read those words on the page.

Same thing with the bloody fight scene in *Kill Bill: Volume Two* when Uma Thurman's character yanks out the eye of Darryl Hannah's character as they're locked in a savage battle. Hannah's character has already lost one eye so this act of violence—having her other eye clawed out of its socket—completely blinds her. And it's depicted in gruesome detail.

It's several degrees less upsetting, but I also cringe when I see the popped-out artificial eye of "Mad Eye" Moody in the Harry

Potter movies. Yes, it's an eye with magical powers and the capability to rotate 360 degrees. That's cute. And kind of funny. But it's not magical to me. Just ugly.

Years ago, during a brief period when I made my living as a yoga teacher, I took a workshop with Lilias Folan, the American matriarch of yoga. Her 1970s-vintage PBS show, *Lilias! Yoga and You,* aired for 500 episodes over three decades. In her signature leotard and waist-length braid, Lilias was a Midwestern housewife introducing hatha yoga to a culture wary of what seemed at the time like a foreign religion or a cult.

Lilias came to Florida once and led a weekend training for yoga teachers. It was the mid-'80s and by that time, she had branched out beyond the traditional yogic fare of asana and pranayama—postures and breathwork. Now Lilias was into something more esoteric.

First, she split the 50 or so of us into two groups and arranged us into concentric circles on the floor of the drafty gymnasium where we had gathered. It was some kind of Greek dance, she explained. As the music started, we moved clockwise and counterclockwise in our circles. At various points the music signaled us to stop and bow to the person opposite us in the other circle. It was an uncomfortable face-to-face moment, but the music quickly moved us on.

Then Lilias upped the ante. She divided us into pairs and told us to sit on the floor opposite our partner. We were cross-legged, hands in our laps, knees brushing against each other's. The exercise was simple. All you had to do was look straight into your partner's eyes, saying nothing. Sit there and stare at each other. In total silence. For five minutes. The quintessential touchy-feely, Esalen-style "soul gaze."

I don't remember Lilias' exact instructions, or how we were supposed to overcome the inevitable awkwardness. I only remember my brain's one-word cry of panic. *Nooooooo!* Don't make me do this! Anything but this! Staring into someone else's eyes, with them staring into mine, is the last thing in the world I want to do. I sat there with my eyes watering, mind churning, heart gasping like a fish flung onto the sand. Those five minutes felt like five hours.

Whenever these things happen—a casual reference to eye injury, a gory movie scene, an eye-gazing exercise—I am plunged into the familiar land of self-loathing. It's a struggle to work my way back to some kind of equilibrium, a place where I can feel reasonably calm and relaxed.

When I became a psychotherapist, I learned about fight-flight-freeze, our innate response to perceived danger. I tell my patients that the brain's limbic system is like a smoke alarm, primed to alert us to any sign of danger. It's helping us protect ourselves from all kinds of threats: scary situations and things that are truly physically dangerous, but also emotional assaults—painful memories, things that make us sad, people who say hurtful things to us. The limbic system helps us decide on an appropriate response: engage in an argument (fight), walk away (flight), or shut down like a scared rabbit (freeze).

It's a highly efficient, ever-vigilant system, but there's one problem: A smoke alarm can be fooled. Sometimes it goes off when there's only a little bit of smoke, not a full-fledged fire. And that's why we can find ourselves in a state of fight-flight-freeze when it's unwarranted, overreacting to something that isn't truly a threat.

When something reminds me of my disability or puts me in a discomforting situation because of my eye, it's not a full fire. But my brain revs into flight mode, anyway. I want to escape. And if I can't escape—for example, if I'm stuck sitting on a gymnasium floor while a stranger peers into my eyes—the brain goes for a different option. Freeze.

This is a sequence anyone with a trauma history knows well. It's also the bread-and-butter of what I see daily in my psychotherapy practice. Let me offer an example. This is a fictitious patient, a composite of several people I've treated in the past, with details from their personal stories blended to protect their privacy. Let's call our imaginary patient Jane Doe.

Jane endured a childhood with multiple traumas. In infancy, she was given up by her biological mother and placed in an adoptive home where she was abused physically, emotionally, and psychologically by her new parents. The environment she grew up in was frequently chaotic and violent. She never knew when one of the dysregulated, heavy-drinking adults around her was going to explode and maybe direct their rage at her. So she learned how to protect herself: stay quiet, not express her own feelings, try not to draw attention to herself. Looking back, Jane can sum it up in one sentence: "I never felt safe."

Almost thirty years later, Jane is a fully functioning adult. But her brain in some ways remains stuck in those early years when she had to be on guard all the time. It constantly scans the environment, putting her limbic system in a chronic state of alertness that's exhausting not only mentally but physically.

As a child, when the abuse was going on, Jane didn't have the fight option. Flight wasn't possible, either. So her go-to was freeze. She remembers how she couldn't even cry when her parents were leveling their rage at her.

The adoptive mom is now an elderly woman who no longer has any control over Jane, but still tries to emotionally manipulate her. And when she does, a specific region of Jane's brain—a small, almond-shaped mass in the medial temporal lobe called the amygdala—registers fear. The whole cascade response begins. The smoke alarm is blaring, even though there's not a fire. *Freeze!*

Interestingly enough, Jane's amygdala responds to other fearful situations—ones that don't involve her parents—with the fight option she couldn't use as a child. For years, she chose jobs that required her to be strong and face down danger. She has worked as a night security guard, a police officer, and the behavioral tech in a hospital psych ward who tackles out-of-control patients. It's as if Jane is experimenting with how it feels to fight back.

Her other tough-guy defense mechanism is sarcasm. It peppers our sessions, especially whenever we touch on painful topics. A caustic remark or a joke ensures that she can avoid expressing the depth of her feelings, that she can stay in a place where she feels safe. Her brain is remembering that in her childhood, expressing feelings was scary and often led to violence.

Some of this is good news: Jane's brain found a way early on to help her cope. It protected the child who felt defenseless. The bad news is that it became, as these things do, a patterned response she carried into adulthood.

This is when I educate my patients about neural pathways. I tell them it's like a trail in the forest. The more you walk that trail, the more cleared it is. It becomes the "easy" way through the woods, so that's the trail you take every time. The patterned response is the neural pathway the brain chooses by habit.

Is there anything that can heal this patterned response? Is there a way to create new, healthier neural pathways? The answer is something amazingly simple: It's your body.

In the past three or four decades, a whole crop of somatic or body-based therapies has emerged. Their premise is that the body/mind system has an innate wisdom and a built-in orientation toward homeostasis. It *wants* to heal itself. That's what I stumbled upon back in the 1980s, when I used my body to help heal the photophobia in my sighted eye.

These somatic or body-based therapies are referred to as "bottom up," in contrast to talk therapy, which is cognitive in nature and thus "top down." They're also sometimes called the "third wave" of psychotherapy—the first wave being the early twentieth-century's Freudian psychoanalysis, and the second wave being cognitive-based methods, which dominated mental health treatment during the second half of the twentieth century.

My training in yoga helped me understand this "bottom-up" approach right away. I already knew the ancient science of pranayama, in which breathwork can produce a state of equilibrium in parts of the body affected by stress: the autonomic nervous system, for example, and the muscular system. Many of the newer body-based therapies use breathwork as an ally.

The concept of bilateral movement is also important. When we walk, for example, our arms and legs are moving in a rhythmical pattern that soothes the brain and switches on the parasympathetic nervous system, the branch of the nervous system responsible for creating the so-called relaxation response. Other examples of bilateral movement are drumming, dancing, and swimming, even something sedentary like knitting, where our hands are moving back and forth in tandem, over and over.

Somatic therapists plug this concept into how we interact with our patients. As soon as I heard about "walk and talk" therapy, I latched right on to it. Walking side by side with my patient, we both feel the calming effects of that bilateral movement and the sensory experience of being outdoors. Also, we're not sitting face-to-face, which makes difficult subjects somehow easier to discuss. A "walk and talk" session feels completely different—refreshing, easy, vital.

The most famous type of bilateral, body-based therapy is EMDR, or Eye Movement Desensitization and Reprocessing. It's a remarkably effective method for processing traumatic memories, by simply having the patient's eyes move back and forth in a patterned way. Early in my therapy career, everyone was jumping on the EMDR bandwagon and my mentor strongly suggested that I train to become a certified EMDR practitioner.

I just couldn't.

When I looked into the training, I learned that part of it involves the therapist becoming a patient. In other words, we ourselves undergo the treatment, with a trainer watching us as our eyes shift back and forth, following their fingers as they move across our field of vision.

That would mean a person looking directly at me, watching my eyes, noticing how one of them doesn't move normally from side to side … and then the conversation we'd have to have about that. The very thought of it all sent chills down my spine. My amygdala fired up, and the smoke alarm in my brain started blaring.

So I missed the EMDR train. And I needed other ways to incorporate somatic therapy into my work. Eventually I found an online training program for therapists offered by a California organization called The Earthbody Institute. Over the course of several months, I studied an emerging field called ecotherapy—therapy anchored in the natural world. It felt so inviting for me, the child who had played by herself in the woods behind our house, the young girl who felt less lonely in the company of trees and sky.

From day one, I fell in love with ecotherapy. It is literally and figuratively well-grounded, with an increasing body of research to back it up. When humans go into nature, our bodies quickly respond with physiological markers of lowering stress response. Blood pressure drops, heart rate slows, the level of cortisol dips. These are automatic effects facilitated by the natural world.

In other words, nature provides the opposite of fight-flight-freeze. A calm amygdala. A quiet smoke alarm. This is why I call the Earth my "co-therapist."

Any time my patients and I go into nature, we're surrounded by soothing shades of green, a color that lies in the middle of the spectrum—signifying balance. The trees around us are not only pumping fresh oxygen into the air we breathe. They're also releasing organic compounds called phytoncides, which bolster our immune system. Meanwhile, our eyes are exposed to the full spectrum of light, which is much healthier for us than the high-energy blue waves we absorb from our digital screens.

The days when I have ecotherapy sessions scheduled are my favorite days of the week. My patient and I walk along trails in a state park or a botanical garden—anywhere we can find the simplicity and solace of nature. We walk, yes, and we talk, but we also pause. During those pauses, I use "invitations" to coax the patient into a deeper relationship with their surroundings.

A typical invitation engages all five senses. Inevitably, the patient finds a metaphor in nature that inspires them, that they can relate to their own struggles. Maybe it's a tree that has grown in a graceful curve around an obstacle, or a stream flowing over rocks. Maybe it's the elemental joy of a bird singing its heart out.

This kind of therapy, with its emphasis on the whole body instead of the eyes, feels like a perfect fit for me. It's also brilliantly simple. A walk in nature. A brain and nervous system at peace, mine as well as my patient's.

Together we forge a new neural pathway through the woods.

Chapter 8

Blindsided

This should be a quick in-and-out, I thought.

As we walked into the Department of Motor Vehicles, I was cheered to see the line wasn't too long. We were there for a simple errand, to change our driver's licenses from Florida to South Carolina. A chore as mundane as any of the others you do when you've moved to a new state.

This DMV office was home turf for me. It's just down the road from the hospital where I was born. This was the town where I injured my eye. This was the community that flooded my family with cards, telegrams and offers of help while I was hospitalized. This was the place where all three churches in town were praying for me.

Now, 45 years later, I'd come back here to live because my husband and I wanted to escape the traffic and heat of Florida. We wanted to live in a smallish, friendly town. We also wanted to be near my parents, who were getting older and could benefit from our presence nearby. It felt good to be back. I was eager to get the driver's license that would identify me as a South Carolina resident once again.

Braving the DMV is never particularly pleasant for anyone, but my first challenge comes at the check-in desk, where they want you to peer into the little machine and read the letters you see on the screen inside. I always have to preface the vision test with, "I can't see out of my right eye, so I'll be reading only half the line."

That announcement usually inspires a quizzical look, but the embarrassment is fleeting. The check-in clerk scribbles something on the paper they hand me, and I end up with a license that has an extra restriction on it. Call it the Monocular Special. I am required to have outside mirrors on my vehicle to augment my less-than-stellar peripheral vision.

(I've never in my life driven a vehicle that didn't have outside mirrors, but I guess that's beside the point.)

As we checked in that day, I was expecting the usual brief set-to at the front desk. Hopefully it would resolve quickly. I made my half-the-line announcement to the clerk. She peered at me over the top of the vision testing machine, which was screwed onto her desk.

"What do you mean?" she said. I swallowed. Here we go.

There were several people in line behind me. Suddenly I was back in third grade, not wanting anyone to know I'm different from everyone else. Trying not to draw attention to myself. Wishing I could disappear.

For a moment, I considered faking it. Telling her I was kidding about not seeing out of my right eye, then making up letters as I "read" the other half of the line. Of course, that wouldn't work. So I repeated my announcement to the clerk. I was trying to keep my voice low. She leaned toward me, frowning.

I could feel the trouble coming. It was a thunderstorm rolling in from a far horizon.

She said something about my needing a letter from an eye doctor. My ears started to buzz. The warning light in my amygdala had blinked on. It was flashing red. The brain, readying for war.

I tried to tell her I just moved here. I didn't have an eye doctor yet. It would take weeks to get in to see someone as a new patient. And I wanted to get my license today. I wanted to get this simple errand done.

She wasn't having it. She hauled herself out of her chair and, without a word to me, lumbered over to one of the "customer support specialists" stationed at the high counter spanning the other side of the room. They huddled in conversation for a minute or two as sweat broke out in my armpits.

She came back, and I heard the words "low vision" in the stream of what she was saying to me. I couldn't hear much else. I was now in full-blown fight-flight-freeze, with an emphasis on freeze. The line of people behind me was growing longer. I heard the door repeatedly swinging open, as more customers came in. Somehow my brain, despite its rising distress, came up with a fact.

"I've been driving for 30 years," I told the woman. "I've been licensed in four states. Texas, North Carolina, Georgia, Florida. This was never a problem anywhere else."

She blinked, unimpressed. "You'll have to get a letter from your eye doctor," she said. "You need to come back later."

I could feel the dismissal. She wanted this problem standing at her desk to move along. She wanted to go back to processing people who aren't problems. People who are normal.

In a lightning-like flash, my freeze switched over to fight. "I need to talk to your supervisor," I said.

I was acutely aware of my husband's physical presence next to me. Jim hates confrontation. I knew he was wishing we could leave. Walk outside, sit in our car in the parking lot, strategize, maybe come back another day. Anything but this escalating situation.

Jim was acquainted with my temper. He knew it can flare when someone blocks me from what I want to accomplish. I do not deal well with being controlled. Never have.

The woman behind the desk sighed. I had messed up her nice, uncomplicated morning. She glanced at the lengthening line behind me, her lips pursed. She got up again, shuffled across the room, and disappeared into an office behind the high counter.

"I'm sorry," I said to Jim. He just smiled at me, that smile he wears when he's hoping things won't boil over, but knowing they probably will. My husband is a peace-loving person. If he had been in my shoes that morning, he'd probably have said something like,

"Okay, this is all very inconvenient. But we'll get a doctor's letter and we'll come back."

He was not in my shoes, though. I was. And inside me a voice was chanting a command: *Don't give up! Don't give up!*

I turned and smiled at the people directly behind us in line. I murmured an apology. They didn't smile back. I was now everybody's problem.

A few minutes later, we were out of the check-in line and standing near the chairs where people sit when they're waiting to be called to the counter—those lucky two-eyed people who passed the vision test with ease and were greenlighted to the next step of the process.

I was now listening to a woman who identified herself as the manager of this DMV office. She wore a name tag. I memorized it. She talked to me slowly, deliberately, as if I were stupid.

"This is a new policy this year," she said. "If someone can't pass the vision test, they need to bring in a letter from an eye care professional that vouches for their ability to drive safely."

She was reciting from a training manual, I was pretty sure. She sounded like a robot.

I repeated everything I told the check-in clerk: I just moved here. I don't have an "eye care professional" yet. It would be inconvenient to go find one and wait to see them. The South Carolina driver's manual says I have ninety days after moving here to get my new license. So here I am, trying to do exactly that. And besides, I have been licensed in several other states. They certified me as safe-to-drive, even as a monocular.

She listened to my speech, but her face was a blank slate. It seemed clear they didn't get a lot of monoculars at this DMV. Like, maybe, never.

"You say you're blind in one eye?" she said.

I was confused. Didn't we already establish that? Didn't I explain that I can read only one half of the line in the machine? And, more importantly, that I can read the other half perfectly fine?

"Yes," I said. "I wear an artificial eye over my blind eye."

I felt like a balloon emptying of air, shrinking into a withered heap of latex.

She pondered for a moment. "Well, you'll have to prove that to me," she said.

My brain exploded in something that felt like a mini-burst of fireworks inside my head. What did she just say?!

"I don't know what you mean."

Actually, I did know what she meant. And now I was scared. Really scared. Like I was in a dark alley, with footsteps behind me. I was about to be assaulted. My body tensed into a fetal position, even though I was still standing.

"If you will take out your false eye and show me that it's blind …" she started.

I looked at Jim. He was helpless. I could see it on his face. He wanted to empower me to decide what to do. He had given this situation over to me. But he was standing close. I felt his support, even through the mounting heat inside me.

Now the fear was morphing into white-hot anger. I was suddenly pissed beyond words. And just as suddenly, I was standing here representing all disabled people everywhere, in every moment when we've been marginalized, inconvenienced, made to feel like a problem, separated from the herd.

Where are our accommodations? Where are my accommodations?

I'm disabled, dammit, and I want my accommodations!

I looked at the manager and I wasn't sure I could get any words out. My throat was clogged with a thick mucus of rage.

"Okay," I sputtered. "But I'm not gonna do that out here in public."

She motioned us toward the office behind the high counter. I followed her, feeling like I might vomit into any nearby trash can. Jim was right behind me. I felt his hand on the center of my back. The touch of love.

How could this be happening? Why wasn't my own word good enough? It always had been, for three decades of driving, in four different states. But somehow, right now, these people in this little town where I was born didn't trust me. Somehow, for some crazy reason, they thought I was trying to scam the system, that I would lie about having a blind eye.

Somehow, right now, I was walking into an office where I was going to do something I would never, but never, do in public. I was going to remove my artificial eye in front of a stranger who had no right to demand this of me.

The sense of unreality wrapped around me like fog. I was walking, but I didn't quite feel it.

The office was a large open space where three other women sat at randomly spaced desks. They looked up with curiosity as the director led me to a spot in the center of the room. Clearly, customers were never brought back here.

A window on the far wall overlooked a paved lot out back with two wooden barricades set a few feet apart—the place where driving test examiners have people demonstrate their parallel parking skills. I don't know why my brain registered that small detail at that moment. Except for the fact that when I was a teenager, I struggled to learn how to parallel park. I delayed going for my first driver's license until I was 17 because I was so nervous about that segment of the road test.

Right now, I would have loved to be out there, showing an examiner what a great parallel parker I had become. That would be a breeze compared to this, to what was about to happen.

"Okay," said the manager. "Take out your eye."

I looked around. The three workers were staring at us, slack-jawed. They had a front row seat.

I was stunned. I thought this woman was going to take me in the ladies' room, for god's sake. Or maybe a storage closet. Nope. She wanted me to do this right here, in front of her and three other people who knew nothing of my situation, who had no idea what was going on. Also in front of anyone else who might happen to walk through this office in the next two minutes. There was not a shred of privacy.

My head started to pound like someone was whacking it with a sledgehammer. I'd never in my life felt such a powerful surge of fight-flight-freeze. But none of those three options were available in that moment. I couldn't fight. I couldn't run. I couldn't freeze.

I lifted my hand to my right eye. In a sweep of the index finger across my eyelid, the prosthesis was out and in the palm of my hand. I was naked in a way that's a million times worse than if I were standing there with no clothes on.

I looked at the manager. I stared at her, full on, the horror-movie ugliness of my blind eye fixed on her. I wanted to burn a hole in this woman's forehead with my gaze. I wanted her to feel pain. Embarrassment. Guilt. Anything, everything. I wanted her to remember this moment for a very long time.

Way back in some remote corner of my mind I was aware, just for a second, that this was awful for her too. That she probably hated ending up in this bizarre situation she didn't think would go this far. That she felt as trapped as I did. The two of us, standing face to face, entangled together in a web of dukkha.

She didn't say a word. Not that I can recall, anyway. Maybe she did say something. Jim later told me she apologized. I didn't hear it. My entire nervous system was on fire. I couldn't hear anything but the roar in my ears.

Five minutes later, my new driver's license was in my hand. The photo was the first one I've ever had on a license where I'm not smiling. My face, caught in the camera's flash, didn't look angry. It didn't look sad. Just blank and expressionless.

Like the face of a dead person, her eyes wide open.

Chapter 9

An Eye for an I

There's one place in the world where I don't mind taking out my eye: the sanctity of an ocularist's office.

That is my safe zone where I'm comfortable and can truly be myself.

It's an astounding experience, sitting there with someone who, I know, has absolutely no question in their mind about why my eye looks the way it does. No judgment, no shock, no suspicion that "Hmm, something's wrong with her eye, but I can't figure out what."

I can't tell you how many people have said that to me, or some version of it, over the course of my lifetime. Hundreds, maybe thousands.

I could tell something was different about your eye, but I never guessed it was blind.

These are almost always kind, caring people who are trying to reassure me. Unfortunately, it doesn't work. A comment like that only reaffirms my perennial fear that others are silently noticing, silently wondering. Even if there's no cruelty involved—and there almost never is—I know, or think I know, that they've honed in on my flaw.

It would be better, frankly, if they asked. Then I could explain. We could get it out in the open and move on. But people are trained to be polite, not to comment on someone's physical features unless it's a compliment. So we don't talk about it.

That silence, sadly, is the disabled person's nemesis. In the absence of feedback about our appearance, we assume the worst. We tell ourselves that everyone can see what's wrong. Everyone thinks we look weird. Everyone is either judging or pitying us.

It's self-absorption at its most negative, rumination with no endpoint.

This internal monologue is the undertone of most every conversation I've ever had with someone I'm meeting for the first time. *Are they noticing?* frets the voice in my head. *What are they thinking?*

Somewhere in adulthood, I learned to ignore that voice and keep plowing ahead. I gave speeches, performed in plays, took a job where I would be meeting new people constantly and interviewing them face to face. I challenged myself to go into situations where people would be staring at me. I gave the voice in my head a new mantra: *Who cares whether they're noticing or not? I've got a life to lead!* Sometimes that internal cheerleading works, sometimes it doesn't.

The only reason I could even attempt things that put me in the public eye was thanks to the skill of ocularists. In my fangirl opinion, these people are the geniuses of the medical world. They're technicians, they're artists, they're compassionate angels. And almost no one knows about them or understands what they do.

In a beautiful combination of science and art, an ocularist creates artificial eyes for people who have lost their sight in one eye due to disease or injury. The custom-made prostheses they craft are amazing simulations of a normal eye. What they do for us monoculars is the difference between disfigurement and normalcy.

I don't think I can overstate what this means to someone like me. If I didn't have this scleral shell snugly inserted in front of my blind eye—this roughly circular, quarter-size piece of acrylic—I couldn't have done half the things I've done in my life.

I couldn't have made those speeches. I couldn't have had a career as a journalist. I wouldn't have had the confidence to date, pursue a romance, or get married. My self-esteem would have been in tatters. My life so much less than what it has been. I think back on those first seven years after my accident—when I was a half-blind child living without a prosthesis, when my disfigured eye was on display to the world, when I hung my head to hide my deformity—and I shudder.

If a house fire ever breaks out at 3 a.m., the one thing I will grab before I run out the door is my artificial eye floating in its little overnight container on the bathroom counter. It's my most prized possession.

From my first prosthesis at age 9 until now in my late sixties, I've had a grand total of five ocularists. I want to salute them by name here: Pauline Long and Walter Burkhardt in Maryland, John O'Donnell in Texas, Randy Minor in Florida, and Emma Boyd in North Carolina. Each one is a hero to me.

Every seven years or so, the scleral shell needs to be replaced. My face has aged, as faces do. My blind eye has shrunk more. The old shell is not a perfect fit anymore. That's when it's time for a replacement. Time to visit the artist who will make my new eye.

Once I'm in the ocularist's office, that safe zone where I can be totally myself, one of the first things the ocularist does is take my prosthesis out of my eye and look it over. They want to see how it can be improved, what kind of adjustments they'll need to make in the new one. And during that process, I'm sitting there naked, my blind eye unclothed and on display.

The ocularist and I are having a conversation, catching up on what's been happening in our lives since we last met. (I can tell you random facts about each of my ocularists—details about their career history, where they've been on vacation recently, their kids' names and ages. We're more than clinician and patient. We're friends.) It bothers me not in the slightest to be having a conversation without my artificial eye in place. The ocularist looks straight at me, making eye contact. No problem. I'm at ease in a way I can never be anywhere else in my life.

Then the work begins on the new eye, and my admiration for this person deepens.

First they make a mold of my eye. After it hardens, they shape and carve the mold, using a palette knife heated over a Bunsen burner. This takes meticulous hand-eye coordination, plus the knowledge of exactly what thickness and shape they want the mold to be so it will hold my eyelid open. Then they disappear into the back lab, where more magic happens.

After a lunch break, they present a cured acrylic shell that's custom shaped to my eye but is blank white. It's time to turn this piece of plastic into an eye.

The ocularist brings out a tiny brush and a paint set that looks disarmingly like a child's watercolors. This is when I find out that the iris of my good eye isn't really brown. It's a mixture of several colors: brown, orange, gray, tan, black, even a touch of green. I watch with fascination as more and more hues are added. The gorgeous, complex art of the human eye.

Within an hour, the ocularist has painted an iris that's a clone of my good eye. Then the shell goes into an electric pressure cooker for an hour or two to harden and set.

For my first few scleral shells back in the '60s and '70s, it took several visits spread over two days to complete this process. Now it's much quicker. Making an artificial eye is still labor-intensive, but the technology has advanced to the point where it can be accomplished in one day. The last time I visited my ocularist, we started at 8:30 a.m. By 2 p.m., I was out the door and on my way home, proudly wearing my brand-new eye.

To co-opt the old adage, a good ocularist is hard to find. The reason? There aren't that many of them. The American Society of Ocularists has only about 200 members, and their annual conferences attract an average of 300 ocularists from around the world. It's a small and select fraternity.

To become an ocularist, the student must earn 750 credits of online study. Then they spend five years or 10,000 hours as an apprentice to another ocularist. That's a lot of training, obviously. Comparable to a medical student's years of study and clinical training.

When I sit across the table from an ocularist, I'm confident this person is highly skilled and deeply dedicated to their craft. That is essential to me. I'm entrusting them with every shred of my self-esteem, and so is each patient who walks in their office.

When I was 14, I wrote a thank-you note to John O'Donnell, the Dallas ocularist who took care of me during my adolescent years. He had just made a prosthesis for me, the second of two I received from him.

I really should be doing my homework right now, I wrote. *But I want to tell you that I am a changed person due to my visits to your office. Yours must be a very satisfying career. To daily make people happy must be an exhilarating experience.*

I remember "Mr. O" as an elfin man, a kind person who took his time with me. He knew how important this painted plastic disk was to my fragile teenage self-image. He knew I'd have my yearbook photo taken soon. I'd be asked to smile into the camera by someone who had no idea what a challenge that was for me. And how that would remind me of the humiliation of all those grade school years, when my photos were taken in profile, to hide the bad eye.

So Mr. O worked hard to make the prettiest, most lifelike eye he could.

A brand-new eye: It's the gift I receive every seven years. All over again.

Chapter 10

Face to Face

I was sitting in the back seat of a car as it rolled along the autumn-gold streets of Birmingham, Alabama. I'd been there two days, on assignment from the Florida newspaper where I worked, the *St. Petersburg Times*. As a feature writer, I was often sent out to spend one-on-one time with someone in order to produce a lengthy profile piece.

In this case, that someone was Emily Lyons. She was the nurse who barely survived a 1998 bombing at the abortion clinic where she worked, one block from the University of Alabama campus. Emily, who was in her early forties, was a former labor and delivery nurse. Earlier in her career, she helped birth hundreds of babies. Then she answered an ad for part-time work in a "doctor's office" that turned out to be a women's reproductive health clinic. The clinic offered general gynecological care, pregnancy tests, birth control—and abortions.

On that day when I rode with her, Emily was in the front passenger seat. Her husband Jeff was driving. His hand rested on the gear shift, Emily's hand on top of his. They were college sweethearts who wed four years earlier, after divorcing their former spouses. The ten months since the explosion at the clinic had been a blur of surgeries, one after another, as doctors tried to repair the horrific damage done to Emily's body.

Despite the ongoing trauma she endured, Emily and Jeff maintained their sense of humor. It was a signature coping mechanism for them. She told me they came up with a name for what happened to her: "BTFU Syndrome"—Blown the Fuck Up. She and Jeff were working on a book about her experience. The title would be *Life's Been a Blast!*.

Since the bombing, Emily hadn't shied away from publicity. She wanted the world to see, in gruesome detail, what happens when extremism descends into violence. She had appeared on *Good Morning America*, *Today*, *CBS This Morning*, *Nightline*, *America's Most Wanted*, *Hard Copy*, and *Larry King Live*. Twice she was featured in *People* magazine. I was one of many reporters asking questions, taking pictures, probing her life. Even so, she welcomed me to spend a couple of days with her.

On that drive, we were headed to New Woman All Women Health Care, so Emily could visit her old co-workers. This wasn't her first time back there since the bombing, but each visit was a fresh reminder of what happened that morning.

Emily had arrived early to open the clinic and was reaching to unlock its front door. About twenty feet away the security guard, an off-duty Birmingham police officer, squatted to look at a strange object on the ground in front of the building. As Emily turned her head toward him to say good morning, their world exploded.

Bomber Eric Rudolph was across the street, watching. He detonated the bomb by remote control.

The police officer was flung into a metal railing and died instantly. Metal shrapnel and roofing nails, hundreds of them propelled at 6,000 feet a second, shot toward the clinic door where Emily stood. She crumpled to the pavement like a rag doll. Paramedics later said they'd never seen anyone survive who had been injured so severely.

Rudolph, the infamous Atlanta Olympic Games bomber, was later convicted of the attack, along with several other bombings. He spent five years hiding in the mountain wilderness of western North Carolina, on the FBI's Ten Most Wanted List, before he was finally arrested. He is now serving four consecutive life sentences at the "SuperMax" U.S. Penitentiary in Colorado, a high-security prison where the country's most notorious and violent criminals are jailed.

The bomb Rudolph planted at the women's clinic in Birmingham tore Emily's body to shreds. More than 25 years later, she still has shrapnel in her muscle tissue that doctors cannot remove. It will be there for the rest of her life, embedded reminders of that day. The story I wrote about her in 1999 started this way:

No matter what you think about abortion, no matter how strong your opinion for or against, the war of words falls silent when you see Emily Lyons.

Her face looks as though it was scrubbed with a malevolent Brillo pad. One cloudy eye doesn't quite match the other one—the one that's gone and replaced by a plastic prosthesis.

The misshapen right hand works to grasp a magnifying glass. The legs, pockmarked with purple scars and skin grafts, are slowly learning to walk again.

This woman has been to hell and back. She is a war casualty.

One reason I was eager to interview Emily was that she lost an eye in the bombing. We had something in common. But I didn't tell her about my eye. Compared to her injuries, mine was so insignificant, so painless, so easily camouflaged. Nevertheless, meeting Emily and telling the story of her suffering was a career highlight for me.

My working life wasn't always so momentous. Early on, I toiled in the typically underpaid, less-than-inspiring jobs most of us start out with. I carefully chose work that didn't involve face-to-face contact. If the job did not require me to encounter people head on, I wouldn't have to feel the distress of wondering if they noticed, or judged.

My first gainful employment, in my teens, was on the production line at a sandwich shop called Sourdough's Emporium. Unlike Subway, this lunch spot stationed its "sandwich artists" back in the kitchen, out of sight from customers. Perfect for me. Even so, my tenure there didn't last long. I was a new and militant vegetarian in those days, so being assigned the task of weighing out slices of salami and ham offended my ethics. I was fired for being a slow and surly meat weigher.

Later on, while living in Florida, I delivered newspapers in the middle of the night—another job that didn't involve much eye-to-eye interaction. Yes, the irony: Long before I had a byline in the *St. Petersburg Times*, I was one of an army of anonymous night-dwellers who delivered that paper to subscribers' homes across five counties. Our shift was seven days a week, rain or shine, no holidays off. Some people do that for years. I lasted one summer.

We carriers would show up at 2:30 a.m. at the distribution center, a cavernous warehouse, to wait for delivery trucks from the printing plant. Once the trucks arrived, we stood at long tables folding newspapers and stuffing them with advertising inserts, then sliding a thick rubber band around each paper. On rainy nights, every single paper had to be slipped into a plastic sleeve. By the end of that process, our hands were smudged black from the ink. Then we packed our vehicles with the booty and drove off into the night, each of us on our assigned route.

As a newbie, I was given what seemed like a great delivery route: the beach towns. I could hardly believe my luck. It was so pleasant, driving along in the dark, no traffic, windows down, warm salt air flowing in. Pre-dawn fishermen standing on the seawall would flag me down and buy a newspaper out of my driver's window. I always carried a few extras for them.

To this day, I can recite the names of all the beach towns I passed through one after another, driving north to south. Indian Rocks Beach, Indian Shores, Redington Shores, North Redington Beach, Redington Beach, Madeira Beach. They lined up shoulder to shoulder along a sliver of land between the Gulf of Mexico and the Intracoastal Waterway.

Quite soon, I found out why none of the other carriers wanted that route. All the beach towns are lined with condominium buildings, and many of those buildings are several stories high. To deliver papers to condos on the upper floors, you can take the elevator—but elevators are slow. And when you're delivering 300 newspapers that are guaranteed to be on people's doorsteps by 6 a.m., you've got to hustle.

So I learned how to stand in a parking lot and toss the newspapers high overhead. With practice, I got pretty good at it. I could hit a doormat on the fifth floor with some accuracy. Except when I was delivering the mammoth Sunday paper. Those beasts, with all their extra sections, weighed an average of six or seven pounds apiece. On Saturday nights, I had to use the elevator.

I would arrive home about 7 a.m. and collapse into bed.

While married to my first husband, I helped him in his lawn care business, which in Florida is a year-round enterprise. We worked long, hard hours in brutal heat and humidity, each of us going through a gallon jug of water a day to stay hydrated. I was lean in those days, very lean.

Many of our accounts were commercial businesses, with lots of shrubbery and dirty parking lots. He operated the big riding mower and did the pruning. My job was to "trim out" with a walk-behind mower, then circle around and around the parking lot pushing a noisy industrial vacuum. By the end of the day, I'd be covered in a fine layer of dust and bits of unidentifiable debris sticking to my sweaty skin.

Occasionally, a customer would ask us to cut down a tree. That was fun. My husband did the scary part, climbing halfway up the trunk with his chainsaw. I stayed on the ground, holding both ends of a fat rope that was looped around the tree. It was important, as the tree fell, to guide it to a place where it wouldn't crush shrubbery or land on a roof or somebody's car. As the final cut went all the way through the trunk, the tree would start to lean and I, maneuvering the rope ends, would pull it down to a safe landing precisely where we wanted the tree to go. Such power! I reveled in my brawn.

After our divorce, I needed a way to make a living, and I needed it fast. Drawing on my existing skill set, I scraped together some income with freelance writing and teaching yoga classes. It wasn't enough, so I enrolled in massage school. That was a six-month undertaking, with the price tag of $2,000. Luckily, the school offered a monthly payment plan.

Once I graduated, got my LMT license, and bought a portable folding massage table, I was ready to take on clients. I made business cards and put out the word that I was available for house calls.

My brief massage career was never what you would call lucrative, but I earned enough to pay the $375-a-month rent on my one-bedroom beach apartment. And it was fun to go into people's homes, set up my table, pop a CD of mellow music into the player, grease my hands with a combination of essential oils, and get to work.

The best part about being a massage therapist was that my clients had their eyes closed. Lying on my table, shrouded in a starched white bedsheet, they were not the slightest bit interested in what my eyes looked like. It was all about my hands, and what kind of magic those hands could deliver. My skill set included a thorough knowledge of what in massage school we called A&P (anatomy and physiology), how stress and injuries knot up muscles, and what to do about that. No one—including me—cared a whit about whether I was seeing my clients with two eyes or one.

Sometime during that period, my freelance writing gig turned into something bigger. It was the late 1980s, pre-Internet, and daily newspapers were flourishing. The magazine job on my resume, from earlier in the '80s, helped me land a post at the *St. Petersburg Times*, which also happened to be the largest paper in Florida. While I was there, the newsroom staff topped 400. Our circulation was around 450,000. The *Times* was a lively, engaging place to work. It had a reputation as "a writer's paper," renowned for grooming Pulitzer winners and reporters who moved on to even larger papers—the *Los Angeles Times, Washington Post, New York Times*.

I could have gone into breaking news and been the beat reporter who shows up at accident scenes or covers county council meetings, the "quick turnaround" writer who churns out several short items a day. But that didn't appeal to me. I wanted to write about people's lives. I wanted to take my time, have longer deadlines, write more in-depth pieces.

So I ended up in newsfeatures. My talented colleagues in that department had enviable, fun jobs: food writer, art critic, book critic, entertainment editor. In those days, large newspapers were so flush, we had both a rock music critic and a classical music critic. In our shoulder-to-shoulder, open walls newsroom, I sat next to a writer who did nothing but review the newest TV shows.

Several of us were general assignment feature writers, the very definition of a plum job. For us G.A. writers, no two days were alike. In the same week, we might write about an alligator farm, hurricane parties, and dolphin research. Florida is a land of strange characters, so a spirit of "anything goes" reigned in our corner of the newsroom. You could pitch a semi-wacky story idea to your editor and if you were convincing enough, the answer would be, "Sure! Go do it."

One of my all-time favorite assignments was tramping through the Everglades with the self-appointed Skunk Ape expert, a guy who used lima beans as bait to try to trap Florida's version of Bigfoot.

In the dawn of the Internet era, when websites were sprouting like mushrooms, I started to wonder if somewhere in the world there was a person named Dot Com. We had no Google back then, so it took quite a bit of digging but finally I found her—a woman in California named Dorothy Comm. Her friends called her Dot. She was seventy-something and not very techno-savvy, but we had a good laugh during our phone interview about her suddenly famous name.

Other stories I wrote were serious, and took me to places where I got a close-up look at the poverty and suffering in developing countries such as Haiti and Cambodia.

Those were the golden days of print journalism when budgets and imaginations were unlimited. I loved it. Every single day I walked into work excited, ready. And every day I met new people, the subjects of my stories. I met them in their homes, on the street and, for one memorable story, in a Lear jet cruising at 50,000 feet. My interviews were almost always done in person, face to face, me asking questions and jotting notes in a reporter's spiral notebook.

Among my famous subjects were psychedelic guru Timothy Leary, wrestler-turned-Minnesota governor Jesse Ventura, and British naturalist David Attenborough. I was having so much fun, and felt so confident in what I was doing, I rarely if ever thought about my eye, or how it appeared to people. I had hit my stride—professionally and personally.

Then came the long, slow rise of the Internet, which launched the long, slow decline of print journalism. By the time my second husband and I moved to South Carolina, many newspaper jobs were in peril. He and I both spent time working at smaller newspapers in the rural area where we'd moved, but that was depressing, underpaid, and dead-end. When Jim was laid off from a mid-size Gannett paper in 2011, we knew our journalism days were over.

So I went back to school, at age 52. It was time to find another career.

For two years, I sat in college classrooms with students 30 years younger than I. After completing my master's degree in mental health counseling, I spent another two years working low-paid jobs to get the clinical experience I needed. I worked in women's domestic violence shelters, as a hospice grief counselor, and at a university campus health center where more than a few of my patients were college students grappling with suicidal urges.

Those were tough years, but important ones. I learned even more than I had as a journalist about the grinding lives so many people lead, the immensity of trauma and suffering that's everywhere. I saw more and more examples of dukkha, the Buddha's First Noble Truth of suffering.

Finally, at the august age of 56, I was ready to launch my own private practice of psychotherapy. I rented an office in a century-old Victorian house alongside two other health care practitioners, a massage therapist and a social worker who practiced something called energy medicine. My cozy one-room space had wooden floors and a bricked-up fireplace. I furnished it with odds and ends I bought on Craigslist and in thrift stories, plus some old pieces "rescued" from my mother's house. You could call the décor eclectic.

As a psychotherapist, I spend my days in intense conversation with people, hour after hour. Six, sometimes seven patients a day. We sit in a room together behind a closed door, face to face. I try hard to create what will feel like a safe zone for my patients. But the fact remains: There's little to no space for emotional escape—for the patients, but also for me. In that room we explore things that aren't talked about elsewhere. We face down the problems as we face each other.

If you had told me when I was a teen that someday in the distant future I'd be making my living staring at people—and being stared at by them—I wouldn't have believed it possible. I would have told you I can't bear having someone look at me for more than a second. Even after I got a prosthetic eye, and even after those prosthetic eyes got better over the years, I've never been comfortable with attention directed at me. I can never quite believe that I look normal. This is how trauma creates indelible personality traits in a person, shaping us as a potter's hands shape clay.

Since the pandemic, I now see my counseling patients either outdoors, for nature therapy, or online. The video sessions started as a response to Covid, when we couldn't see patients in person. But I discovered I love doing telehealth, a form of therapy that makes mental health care even more accessible. My patients enjoy the convenience of having a counseling session from the privacy and comfort of their home, and it's the same for me. We save gas and we save time.

My "commute" is walking down to a spare room in the basement of my house where my laptop and a pair of headphones await me. I can be upstairs folding laundry or feeding the cat, and five minutes later I'm downstairs clicking into session with my next patient. I'm almost always barefoot, and often wearing pajama pants. As long as I look professional and well-groomed from the waist up, we're good.

Even online, my patient and I maintain intense eye-to-eye contact. They're on my screen and I'm on theirs—actually, much closer-up than when we were sitting six feet apart in my office. The thing is, when I'm with a patient and we're talking about their issues, I am 100 percent present for that. There's absolutely no time or space for my mind to be worrying about my eye.

The blessing of psychotherapy, for me as the therapist, is that I've learned how to get outside of myself. I have to. I'm working on others' trauma and in so doing, I set aside my own.

Chapter 11

Ten Thousand Joys, Ten Thousand Sorrows

Spirituality, for me, has been a long and winding road. It's a journey that led me through the desert of trauma to a flowering oasis.

The twists and turns began when I was 15, standing in church between my parents as we sang a hymn. We were at Highland Park Presbyterian in Dallas, one of those mammoth churches with an ornate stone façade reminiscent of Gothic cathedrals in Europe.

I think that's where my love of church sanctuaries blossomed. To this day, I am drawn to houses of worship. It doesn't matter what faith tradition they serve. If it's a place where people gather for spiritual communion, I am captivated.

The silence in those buildings. Polished floors and wooden pews. Sunlight refracting through stained glass. The scent of the sacred. I love it all.

Which makes what happened that Sunday morning in Dallas all the more surprising. In a single moment, I left behind my religious upbringing. I wish I could remember what hymn we were singing.

What I do remember is that a powerful awareness came over me, quite suddenly.

A thought fell into my mind, crystal-clear and unapologetic: *This isn't for me. I need something else.*

Maybe that revelation was simply teenage rebellion. Maybe it was curiosity. Or maybe it was a genuine spiritual awakening—not full-blown, not informed by years of practice and study, but the initial spark of that "something else."

I kept going to church, however. There wasn't much choice as long as I lived under my parents' roof. Weekly worship was on their list of things good people do. You show up on Sunday, you listen to the sermon, you write a check and drop it into the offering plate as it's passed from hand to hand along your pew. The women of the church join a circle. The men serve as deacons. Children dutifully memorize the questions and answers of the catechism. You do it all because … well, you just do it.

As soon as I left home, though, my church-going days were over. During my freshman year of college, I became a vegetarian—another decision that couldn't be actualized until I left home. That was the beginning of an ethical search, a hunt for what my own values would be. That first step, giving up meat, had a simplistic base: I loved animals so I didn't want to eat them. The decision had simmered in me since childhood.

At age 8 or 9, I caused waves at the Thanksgiving table for anthropomorphizing the turkey—in front of guests, no less. As

Mother proudly presented the roasted bird, laid out on her fanciest platter, I interrupted the oohs and aahs by announcing that this was "Henry," and I was sorry he had lost his life for the dubious cause of starring in our holiday dinner.

I quickly learned to keep my thoughts on meat-eating to myself.

By the time I was living in a mountain log cabin in my early twenties, the spiritual search was widening. One after another, I sampled a smorgasbord of faith (and non-faith) traditions. The restlessness of the quest never let me pause for long.

I had an agnostic period, an atheist period, a pantheist period, a Wiccan period, and a Druid period, plus a brief flirtation with Native American spirituality. I dabbled in Tarot and the Tao Te Ching. I threw runes and had my astrological chart drawn. I visited a past-life regression therapist, who delivered the startling news that I was once a reindeer herder in Lapland.

I'm sure it was sad and baffling for my parents, watching me drift further and further from the religion they reared me in, but I couldn't help it. I was just so curious about so many things. Other avenues were opening, and I wanted to explore every one of them.

There was also that streak of rebelliousness, which arose when I realized that thanks to my eye injury, I was permanently different from everyone else, with a capital D. As I moved into adulthood, that Differentness became a guiding principle for me.

During my bout with photophobia, the search veered in a more easterly direction as I cast about for a healing practice that might help me. That's when I discovered the disciplines of hatha yoga and meditation. In 1984, I spent a month living in a tent at an ashram in the Bahamas. I wanted to become a yoga teacher, so I signed up for an intensive training program that offered certification in the ancient Sivananda lineage. Little did I know I was enlisting in yoga boot camp.

We ate only two meals a day—meatless, of course—and sweated through three-hour marathon yoga sessions, morning and afternoon. Attendance at pre-dawn Sanskrit chanting was required. We also trained in the Hindu practices of *kriya,* or internal cleansing. One of those, called *sutra neti,* was designed to purify the nasal passages.

Each of us was given a long, narrow strip of cheesecloth. Then we waded from the beach into the Atlantic and soaked our cheesecloth in the warm saltwater. Sutra neti involved threading the wet cloth up your nostril until it came out through your mouth. The experience was every bit as gag-inducing as you might imagine. I remember a lot of retching into the ocean.

By the end of the month, I had earned certification as a Sivananda yoga teacher. And lost 20 pounds.

※

Then came my serendipitous discovery of Theravada Buddhism, the day a wizened monk in saffron robes appeared on my doorstep in Florida and performed a five-minute wedding ceremony.

As my new husband and I explored further, I felt more and more at home on the path of Dhamma. The Buddha's teachings about dukkha made sense to me. They aligned with what I'd already learned from my early-in-life experience of pain and suffering.

Our years of hosting meditation retreats at Bodhi Tree Dhamma Center were a time of rich immersion in the spiritual world. With Buddhism, I had found a practice that centered on sitting in silence, eyes closed. What a welcome refuge that was.

As we sat together in meditation, each of us on our own cushion, I was no different than anyone else. It didn't matter what my eye looked like—or what anyone else's physical flaws might look like. As soon as our eyes closed, we were all the same. Meditators sitting together, the *sangha* or community of practitioners. I fell into company with others in a profound and sacred way that did not reopen old wounds. Sangha became my sanctuary.

There's a well-known Buddhist story about Ananda, the Buddha's attendant and right-hand man. Many of the Buddhist *suttas*, or sermons, start with Ananda asking his teacher a question. In this case, Ananda said to the Buddha that he thought sangha, the community of noble practitioners, is "half of the holy life."

The Buddha's response was swift, and surprising.

"Do not say that, Ananda! Do not say that! Noble companionship is the *whole* of the holy life."

Another way that Buddhism fits me like a glove is its emphasis on mental development, or *bhavana*. When I sit as part of a sangha, alongside my companions on the spiritual path, we are practicing inner vision. What's important is not the world around us, the world of physical reality we see with our eyes. During meditation, we focus on the inner landscape, a place where mind awaits our exploration. A world where we study the source of suffering. And a person doesn't need two eyes to explore that world.

During the dark years after the collapse of my first marriage, I found comfort in my deepening relationship with the Buddhist meditation master named Venerable Henepola Gunaratana. To his followers and students, Gunaratana is known as "Bhante G." *Bhante* is pronounced BAHN-tay. It's an honorific given to Buddhist monks, much like "Reverend" for Christian pastors.

In the late 1980s, soon after my divorce, I started going to Bhante G's newly established forest monastery and meditation center in rural West Virginia. It was called Bhavana Society.

Each time I went there, I'd stay in a *kuti*, a one-room hut modeled after traditional kutis at monasteries in Asia. At Bhante G's center, the kutis are scattered through the woods, each one occupying its own private zone of solitude.

Kutis are bare bones. There's no electricity, no plumbing. Heat comes from a mini-woodstove. You have a plywood bed with a thin foam mattress and blanket, a chair, and a small porch for walking meditation. Nothing else. It's just you the seeker, and the silence.

Whenever I visit Bhavana Society, I choose the kuti that's farthest from the others, deep in the forest where I know I won't be disturbed. There I can meditate to my heart's content, visited only by an occasional deer wandering past in the moonlight. Nowhere else do I feel the peace that wraps around me in that tranquil place.

Bhante G became a Buddhist monk at age 12, ordained at a village temple near his birthplace in the jungles of Sri Lanka. His entire life has been devoted to practicing and teaching Dhamma. The purity of that calling, and his unstinting dedication, appealed to me immensely. I also grew to love Bhante's practical nature, the way he can relate to us "householders" even though he has been a monastic for 80-plus years.

In his youth, Bhante served missionary stints in India and Malaysia, including a time working with the Untouchables. In 1968 he came to America to become the new head of a Buddhist temple in Washington, D.C. He mastered English, earned a PhD. in philosophy at American University, and has written more than a dozen books, including the beloved bestseller *Mindfulness in Plain English*.

In the wake of the Vietnam War, the U.S. Department of State invited him to minister to thousands of Asian refugees who had ended up in Florida. Later in life, he established a scholarship fund in Sri Lanka that provides free education for impoverished children from villages like the one where he was born.

In Bhante G, I see the flowering of *metta* or lovingkindness, the beautiful embodiment of a life spent in service to humankind. He is my inspiration, my spiritual father. And my spiritual home is his home. At Bhavana Society, he oversaw the construction of a large meditation hall that is the heart of the monastery. Its curved wood arches remind me of the ribs of a whale, sheltering the enormous bronze Buddha that sits beneath a stained-glass window. Whenever I slip off my shoes and walk into the great silence of that room, my old love of cathedrals and sacred spaces soars to its apex.

In August 1988, I took part in Bhante's first-ever Eight Lifetime Precepts retreat. He invented this ceremony to address laypersons' desire to make a deeper commitment to the Buddhist path, without having to ordain as a monk or a nun. Bhante took the standard set of five precepts, which lay Buddhists recite daily, and expanded them to eight:

I undertake the precept to abstain from taking life.
I undertake the precept to abstain from taking what is not given.
I undertake the precept to abstain from sexual misconduct.
I undertake the precept to abstain from false speech.
I undertake the precept to abstain from harsh speech.
I undertake the precept to abstain from malicious speech.
I undertake the precept to abstain from useless speech.
I undertake the precept to abstain from intoxicating drinks and drugs causing heedlessness.

For that inaugural Eight Lifetime Precepts retreat, a couple dozen of us gathered in the meditation hall at Bhavana Society.

Wearing white, the traditional color of lay renunciates in the Theravada Buddhist tradition, we knelt before Bhante on the hard floor. With palms pressed together in front of our hearts, we bowed three times—once for the Buddha, once for the Dhamma, and once for the Sangha. This is the traditional opening of any Buddhist ceremony: honoring the Triple Gem.

One by one we chanted our new set of precepts in both Pali and English, and received Bhante's nod of blessing. Then he gave each of us a name in Pali. Mine was Madhavi, "the wise one." That meant more to me, perhaps, than any honor I've received in my life.

When I remarried, my second husband was keen to learn meditation. We started a small weekly sitting group called Circle of Vipassana. Then Jim joined me on a visit to Bhavana Society and peppered Bhante G with questions about Buddhist concepts. Before long, the two of us were hosting retreats just as I'd done years before. Each time, Bhante would fly to Florida and we'd head to a rural conference center rented for the occasion.

For one retreat, I had the wild and somewhat ill-advised idea that instead of going to a rural center, we could paddle kayaks out to a barrier island accessible only by boat. It would be a nature adventure as well as a spiritual retreat. We rented three condo buildings on the island that were clustered together. Two buildings would house the participants. The third building would serve as communal dining hall and meditation space.

The retreat's opening day turned out to be stormy. Instead of kayaking out to the island, we had to hire a fishing skiff to carry us there. As whitecaps bounced the boat up and down and gusts of wind blew salt spray into our faces, Bhante confessed to me that he has a fear of water due to a near-drowning experience in his youth. I was horrified that I'd subjected him to this, but I also knew Bhante's natural equanimity could sustain him through much worse than a bumpy boat ride.

One of the best features of a retreat with Bhante G was the Q&A period after evening meditation. I would set out a small box with a slot in the top, so meditators could submit their questions on slips of paper. One by one, Bhante would pull questions from the box. Sometimes his answer would include stories from his life. Bhante is a gifted storyteller with great comedic timing, even in his second language. Often the meditation hall rocked with laughter as Bhante spun his tales.

I told Bhante I thought he should compile those stories into a book, and I offered to help him write it. He was reluctant, worried that writing about oneself was unseemly for a monk who practices selflessness and non-attachment to the ego. We had several conversations before I could convince him his life story would be valuable to readers. I told him that if we were honest about his life, and didn't spare the details, it could be powerful inspiration for anyone struggling along a spiritual path.

Once he agreed to the project, we sent e-mails back and forth for several months as he shared memories and I strung them together into a narrative. The result was *Journey to Mindfulness: The Autobiography of Bhante G.* Wisdom Publications, the Buddhist press in Boston that publishes all of Bhante's books, released the first edition in 2003.

Ten years later, when Bhante was well into his eighties, he and I had some memorable conversations about aging and death. Soon after my mother died in 2016, I went to Bhavana Society for a period of retreat. Autumn leaves spiraled to the monastery grounds as Bhante and I talked about impermanence and he reflected on his own advanced age. I realized we had more good material for the autobiography, so I suggested we release a new edition, bringing readers up to date and offering more teachings. I wrote several new chapters, this time with Bhante expressing his thoughts on what Buddhism teaches us about how to face the inevitable challenges of old age.

The updated edition of the book ends with Bhante's words about death: "*It's nothing strange, nothing unfamiliar. Just the truth of impermanence. And we must familiarize ourselves with the truth. Only then, finally then, will there be an end to our fear of death. Only then will our suffering cease.*"

After decades of immersion in Buddhist practice, having stumbled onto this path by chance as a young person, my gratitude is vast and deep. I honestly don't know how I would have lived my life without the Buddha's practical and profound teachings on dukkha and impermanence, his brilliant blend of compassion and wisdom. Without those gifts, I would have struggled to make sense of the world, the *"why?"* of trauma, the dispiriting experience of living with only one eye, in a body that isn't quite complete.

Once I came to understand the concept of karma, the immutable law of cause and effect, I could begin to sort out what happened to me at age 2. It wasn't some injustice that rained on me randomly. It wasn't even a tragedy, really. It was simply the lawful unfolding of causes and conditions. Exactly like everything that happens to us, good or bad. The things we want to experience and the things we *don't* want to experience. Our successes, our heartbreaks, our hopes and our dreams. Everything.

There's an old Taoist phrase I love. It's often repeated by Buddhist teachers. This life, they say, holds "ten thousand joys and ten thousand sorrows." We cannot have it any other way. And in our core, of course, we know that. We see the truth of it with our own eyes—blind or not.

Ten thousand joys, ten thousand sorrows.

Chapter 12

A Bird Glowing with Light

My plane arrived in late afternoon at the tiny Mandalay airport.

Because of flight delays that started way back in Tampa at the beginning of this journey, I was 24 hours behind the other meditators I was supposed to meet here. The plan was for us all to ride together to the retreat center, here in the Sagaing Hills of central Burma. When I didn't show up on the appointed day, the other meditators had no choice but to go without me.

So here I was, all alone, standing with my suitcase in a dusty courtyard outside the terminal—if you could call it a terminal. It was a flimsy wooden building about the size of your average convenience store in America, leaning slightly in one direction as if it were uncertain whether it could remain standing much longer. The two workers who met my plane were now padlocking the front door. Clearly, this had been the last arrival of the day and they were ready to go home.

I had no idea how to get to the retreat center and no one around spoke English. All I had was my religious visa, a document giving me permission to enter the country of Burma (now known as Myanmar) and spend a month studying Buddhist meditation. When I went through immigration a few hours earlier, in the capital city of Rangoon (Yangon), the armed soldiers patrolling the airport frowned at my documentation but waved me through.

The visa was written in the lovely, rounded Burmese script that looks like calligraphy. I had no idea what it said, other than my name. I could only hope that somewhere on that document were two words: *Kyaswa Monastery.* My destination.

A small cluster of men standing outside the terminal in Mandalay was having an animated discussion. Each man wore a button-down shirt tucked neatly into a checkered *longyi*, the ankle-length wraparound skirt that is traditional dress for Burmese men. They punctuated their debate with regular pauses to spit red streams of betel juice into the dirt at their feet. The shimmering heat, along with jet lag from a 45-hour trip through eight time zones, had turned me into a wilted flower. It's hard to say which was more tired: my brain or my body.

I guessed the men's debate involved who would drive the foreigner where she wanted to go. At least I hoped that's what they were debating. With a nervous smile, I handed my visa to one of them. I was counting on the fact that I was a religious pilgrim to keep me safe. After more discussion, they seemed to come to an agreement. One of them, a younger man, grabbed my suitcase and slung it into the trunk of his battered white car.

"I take you," he said, motioning me into the back seat. I climbed in, feeling like Miss Daisy with her chauffeur. The two of us in one vehicle, from vastly different worlds.

Our car careened onto a two-lane blacktop and within less than a minute, we were maneuvering between dual rivers of movement that streamed along the dirt shoulders on both sides of the road. People were walking with bundles of firewood on their heads, pedaling rusty bicycles, steering wooden carts pulled by oxen. Whole families were squeezed onto single-engine motorbikes, a baby perched between the handlebars. Other motorbikes were stacked high with wooden crates full of squalling piglets.

Every so often my driver would swerve around an open-air jitney bus that had stopped to discharge passengers. Each jitney we passed was packed with human beings: standing on the back bumper, dangling from the sides, and perched on the roof. Wedged into the crowd on one bus was a pair of Buddhist monks—shaven heads, bare feet, orange robes.

I blinked, and blinked again. The colors were vivid, the noise intense. The dust kicked up by all this human-animal traffic came rolling in the open windows of our car. As my senses struggled to take it all in, my brain started to register that I had arrived in a distant land, a world on the opposite side of the planet from home. The feeling was one of wandering onto a movie set with perfectly costumed extras walking around. It was overwhelming, and surreal.

Eventually the road opened onto a vast plain, with intensely green rice fields stretching to the horizon. In the distance, I could see whitewashed concrete domes of Buddhist stupas dotting the landscape. That pierced my heart with joy. For so long I had wanted to come to a Theravada Buddhist country, a place where the ancient teachings of Dhamma are embedded in the culture and history. I had longed to visit such a place as this, where I could immerse myself in a practice that had flourished here for a thousand years.

And now … I had arrived.

By the time our car pulled up in front of the monastery, or what I hoped was the monastery, we'd been driving half an hour. The lettering on the iron gates was all Burmese script. No English anywhere.

"This the one," said my driver. He got out and retrieved my bag from the trunk.

I had no idea how much this trip should cost, and I had no Burmese *kyat* on me. I asked the driver if he could take U.S. dollars. He said yes. I asked him how much.

"You choice," he said, casting his eyes down at the rubber sandals on his feet.

I handed the driver a $10 bill. He looked at it with wonder, turning it over and over in his hands as if it were a bar of gold. Evidently that was enough. He smiled at me, nodded, and got back in his car. In a cloud of dust he was gone and I stood with my suitcase at the bottom of a steep concrete walkway.

Kyaswa is a traditional Asian meditation center: high and austere, a cluster of stone buildings perched on limestone cliffs overlooking the Irrawaddy River. Silence and heat drape the dusty grounds. Since its founding in the 14th century, the monastery has been funded entirely by local villagers who offer regular *dana*, or donations. Two years before my arrival, Westerners like me had started venturing there every winter to attend the annual one-month retreat.

There is no set fee for retreats at Kyaswa. Visiting meditators are simply invited to offer dana on a freewill basis. This is how it works in traditional Buddhist cultures. The Buddha said you cannot put a price on something as precious as the Dhamma. Everyone contributes as much as they're able, and as much as they feel the teachings are worth to them. Somehow, there are always enough donations to maintain the monastery. It's the opposite of a capitalist system, with its set prices and profit incentives.

For his opening talk that first night, the Sayadaw, or abbot, sat cross-legged on a low wooden chair in the meditation hall, holding a ceremonial round fan in front of him, the translator on his right.

About twenty of us *yogis* sat on neatly arranged rows of cushions on the floor—men on the left side of the room, women on the right.

Sayadaw told us a Burmese legend about a bird that lands in a tree glowing with light. As it sits in the tree, the bird also begins to glow.

"By coming to this sacred place that glows with the light of Dhamma, you too will glow," he said.

Those words would sustain me all the way to the end of the retreat.

We meditators were housed in spartan one-room *kutis* scattered along footpaths that wound all over the mountain. There was intermittent electricity, no air conditioning or fans, and fetid water pumped from the river up to a purifier near the kitchen where we could fill our water bottles. We were warned to wash our hands frequently and not to touch our eyes or mucus membranes. I lived in constant concern about my good eye, hoping it wouldn't get infected. I knew that medical care was far away.

Halfway through the retreat, an army of ants invaded my kuti—despite my care not to keep any food there. Mosquitoes were omnipresent. They arrived each day as darkness fell. I would lie awake and listen to them swarm outside the net that shrouded my bed. If we walked anywhere on the grounds after dusk, I had to drape a shawl over my head.

For several weeks, life was nothing more than the prescribed routine of retreat: rising in predawn darkness, bucket showers, group meditation, solo meditation, and every other day a Dhamma sermon delivered by Sayadaw, in Burmese, with the translator sitting at his feet. On alternate days, one of the two English-speaking meditation teachers who were hosting the retreat would offer a talk of inspiration and encouragement. Some afternoons the grounds would echo with the soprano sing-song of boy monks as they chanted traditional verses from the Pali canon.

As at any traditional Theravada Buddhist retreat, we were strongly advised not to "entertain" ourselves with reading, writing, or conversation. Nothing should distract us from the business at hand: examining the contents of our minds and striving for equanimity. We lived in a sangha of silence and deep practice.

At mealtimes we walked single file in a long line to the open-air dining hall where a buffet of unfamiliar and delicious food was laid out on low tables, always accompanied by a tureen of white rice and a pot of tea. We sat on the floor to eat.

On our way to breakfast every morning at 5:30, the villagers who were offering that day's food would kneel on the ground alongside our path, their heads bowed and palms pressed together in front of their chests. Yellow gold circles of a fragrant paste called *thanakha* decorated their cheeks. It's a Burmese tradition that signifies devotion and also provides a cooling, UV-resistant balm for the skin.

Their reverence, bowing as we walked past and offering us food, was a lovely demonstration of a millennia-old tradition in Asian Buddhism. Laypeople and monastics have a deeply interdependent relationship: Laypeople provide material sustenance to those living a religious life; the monastics provide blessings and Dhamma instruction to laypeople. It is a merit-making activity for laypeople to provide food, money, and other requisites to a monastery.

Laypeople also helped maintain the Kyaswa grounds. Every afternoon, two women from the village would appear in the sandy courtyard near my kuti. Using handmade straw brooms, they set to work sweeping up leaves and other debris. This usually happened during the drowsy hour after lunch, when we yogis were free to rest and escape the heat.

As I lay on my pallet in a pool of sweat under the mosquito net, I'd hear it: the rhythmical *scritch ... scritch ...scritch* of their brooms on the dirt. A pause, then again: *scritch ... scritch ... scritch*. The sole sound in a deserted courtyard.

Steadily, the song of the brooms coaxed my mind into a state of exquisite focus. Eventually all I could hear was that *scritch ... scritch ... scritch*. It filled my ears, my brain, my heart, every cell of me. I knew nothing but the sound of brooms sweeping.

Thanks to round-the-clock meditation, my brain had become like one of the earthen water jars outside the kitchen, emptied of its contents. My awareness was free—blissfully free—to rest on *scritch ... scritch ... scritch.* As my ears received the sound, my mind also received it. Pure perception and nothing else; no labeling, no judgment, no thoughts or opinions. No yearning for some other experience. Only the sound itself, arriving in the same moment at two "sense doors"—ear and mind.

The experience was thrilling in its simplicity, its absolute perfection.

That evening I half-ran, half-skipped to my daily meeting with Michele McDonald, one of the Western meditation teachers leading us. I was an excited child, eager to report my breakthrough.

"That's concurrence," Michele said, with a smile. "Perception and awareness happening concurrently. The knower and the object merging in one single moment. Perfect mindfulness."

We both knew this wasn't enlightenment. I hadn't completely pierced the veil of delusion. This was only one step on a long, arduous journey toward what Buddhists call "awakening." But it was something. It was a flash of lightning, a glimpse, the dawning of an understanding.

Each morning during the month I lived at Kyaswa, I opened the faded wood shutters on the back wall of my kuti. There was no window glass, no screen, just a large open-air rectangle. And there, inches away, was a rock wall, the mountainside that rose directly behind my kuti. It was solid, gray, an impenetrable barrier.

On the hard days, when resistance was strong and my meditation practice faltering, on the stifling hot afternoons when I wondered why I had flown halfway around the world to come to this silent place, I would look at that limestone wall and think, *I'm climbing. Toward the top. Got to make it.*

A spider lived on that wall. Every day, I watched her move about. Mostly she seemed to be climbing the rock face, higher and higher, but she was in no hurry. I felt a connection with her. Both of us were striving for something, creeping toward a goal. In homage to her persistence, to our shared efforts, I gathered fallen flowers from the plumeria tree growing in the hard earth outside my kuti. The blooms were tiny and white, with a divine fragrance. They seemed to symbolize purity. Reverently I lined them up on the windowsill each day—an offering to my spider friend and her climb. Our climb.

The last morning of my month at Kyaswa, I opened the shutters and there was the spider, clinging to the wall far above the height of my head. She had reached the top. I had reached the end of the retreat.

I put out my hand toward the wall. As my fingertips touched it, pieces of rock crumbled and rained to the ground in a cascade of pebbles and limestone dust. I had to smile. This thing I had been climbing in my mind for all those weeks was not as solid or impenetrable as I'd thought. It was fragile and insubstantial. Illusory. Like the whispers of trauma that haunt our minds.

For that moment I was a bird, perched in a tree glowing with light.

Chapter 13

Noble Silence

We're walking on a mountain trail, fifteen of us. I'm at the front of the line. Bringing up the rear is our "sweep," the woman who volunteered to carry the first aid kit in her daypack. Normally, a group this size would make a substantial amount of noise as we hike through the forest. Not us. The only sounds this morning are the *tea-kettle* trill of a Carolina wren and the crunch of our footsteps.

Before we started our walk, I passed out little stickers to everyone and we patted them into place on our T-shirts and jackets. Each sticker displays two words in bold black letters: SILENT HIKER. If we pass other people on the trail, hopefully these stickers will explain why we don't say good morning.

For this hour in the woods, we won't be greeting others. We won't discuss the weather or politics or our kids. If there's a pretty wildflower or an interesting tree stump by the side of the trail, no one will exclaim over it. Each of us walks in our own capsule of quiet. We have chosen Noble Silence.

Ten years ago, when I started leading what I call "silent hikes," I wasn't sure anyone would show up. Who'd want to walk in the woods with a group of people and not say a word the whole time? What's the point of that? And it's true: Some people wrinkle their noses when I explain the concept. Most folks on a nature outing enjoy the conversation with their companions as much as they enjoy the scenery.

To my surprise and delight, our first silent hike filled to capacity—and that's what happens nearly every time I offer one. Four times a year, near each equinox and solstice, I choose a different trail and put the word out to my mailing list. Those four Saturday mornings are perhaps my favorite days of the year. I don't charge a fee for the silent hikes because I'm sure I enjoy them as much as my guests do. And of course, walking together in a single-file line is yet another activity I can take part in without worrying whether someone notices an oddness about my eye.

Time after time, there's a core group of regulars who join the silent hike. Some are meditators attracted by the idea of bringing their practice into the woods. Others, the curious first-timers, see it as an intriguing challenge: Can they survive an hourlong hike without talking? Some people show up simply because they need a break from their noisy, jam-packed lives and a quiet walk in the woods sounds pretty good.

As we gather at the trailhead, I explain the concept of Noble Silence—how it's a gift we give ourselves. It means we can be in congenial company with others but don't have to make polite chit-chat. We can experience human connection without the banal *blah-blah-blah*.

I also tell the hikers how I borrowed this concept from meditation retreats. I suggest that being among others without having to speak or interact can be pleasant. I assure them that even though the silence might feel awkward at first, within a few minutes they'll relax into it. Then I tantalize them by hinting that their experience of the forest will be richer when they're not distracted by conversation. They'll notice more colors and textures. They'll hear more birds and squirrels. They'll spy more insects. They'll fully appreciate the aroma of the air, the sunlight on their skin.

I encourage them to take their first step onto the trail as if they're a wild animal—senses alert, receptive, quivering. And then we start out, a single-file line of quiet, expectant creatures.

The interesting thing about Noble Silence is that it's not something foreign, a contrived practice we do only during a meditation retreat or a silent hike. It's really our natural state. Before humans had language, we had wordlessness. Choosing to walk or sit in silence, even for a few minutes, is returning to our roots.

Every time meditators settle onto our cushions, we sink into the familiar world of silence. It's there waiting for us, once the mind grows calm and concentration settles on one object. For Vipassana meditators, that object is the noiseless rhythm of breath, the soft, dependable in-and-out of our life force. For however long we sit on that cushion, we dwell in silence. We savor silence, we're supported by silence. The silence invites us to journey inward and explore.

Of course, the truth is that silence is rarely a pure absence of sound. When we sit to meditate, there are external noises: someone else in our house, walking from room to room; a car horn or a siren in the street; a bird singing in a tree outside the window. Our own bodies also generate sounds: a rumbling stomach, the rush of a sigh escaping our lips, soft swishing of fabric as we slide our legs into a more comfortable position.

In Vipassana, the kind of meditation I've practiced for 40-some years, our training is to receive any and all sounds impartially, without judgment or analysis. We resist the instinct to identify what the sound is, and whether it's a pleasant sound or an unpleasant sound. Instead, we repeat a one-word mental note: "Hearing ... hearing." Just hearing. The naked experience of a noise presenting itself at the sense door of ear. Sounds come, and they go. Meanwhile, we soften into the ever-present silence that contains it all.

My first taste of silence came on a concrete stoop in front of a duplex in Sioux Falls, South Dakota. It was the home of my maternal grandparents. Every summer, we spent three weeks there—my mother, brothers, and I. Dad drove us there from South Carolina in the family station wagon, then he went back home to work.

My grandfather's name was Henry, but we grandkids called him "Bapa," pronounced BAH-puh. By the time I knew him, when I was old enough to really know and appreciate him, Bapa was in his late seventies. His movements were calm and deliberate, his voice soft. He had the patience of an ocean. Bapa had made his living as a druggist. My mother remembered him working long hours at his pharmacy, all through her childhood. She and her sister would sit at small round tables in the soda fountain side of the store, sipping ice cream floats and waiting for their dad to clean up and close.

Bapa's true joy was the outdoors. Whenever we visited, he took my brothers pheasant hunting and ice fishing. I was much younger, and a girl. So he taught me other things: how to "snap" the snapdragons in my grandmother's flower garden. How to notice the coo of the mourning doves that nested in their yard.

My best Bapa memory is sitting next to him on those front steps, waiting for the squirrels. He always had a handful of peanuts in the shell, and he'd show me how to lay them out in a line along the sidewalk in front of us.

"You have to be still," he told me. "And we need to stay quiet so the squirrels won't be afraid to come close." Neither of us would have called it Noble Silence back then, but that's exactly what we were practicing.

Recently I've been studying silence in a different way, researching how other people in other fields work with sound—and the absence of sound. In 1952, composer John Cage stunned and bemused the music world with his composition for solo piano titled *4:33*. It's a piece in three movements, and the entire thing is four minutes and 33 seconds long. If you watch a video of one of the performances, you'll see the pianist walk onstage, sit at the piano and … do nothing. For four minutes and 33 seconds there is absolute silence, other than the random sounds coming from the audience—a cough or a whisper, occasional nervous rustles. Cage is asking his audience to listen to something extraordinary, something not normally considered interesting or beautiful. And the fact that ambient noise interrupts the silence, for Cage, was an essential part of the experience.

Gordon Hempton discovered much the same thing, in nature. Hempton is an audio ecologist who searches for naturally quiet places all over the world, places where human-made noise is scarce or even nonexistent. He estimates there are fewer than ten such places in the United States. As you can guess, those places are far from urban sprawl, far from the flight path of airports. Hempton goes to these places—he calls them One Square Inch of Silence—and he records the natural sounds there: birdsong, flowing water, wind in the trees, and maybe, hopefully, a moment or two of absolute silence. He has discovered that, paradoxically, silence is far from an empty void.

"Silence is not the absence of something," Hempton says. "It's the presence of everything." I don't know whether Hempton is a meditator, but right there he perfectly describes the experience of meditation.

A few years ago, I visited Muir Woods National Monument in California. That's the place where ancient redwoods hold court.

Silent, majestic trees as tall as skyscrapers. They're breathtakingly huge. As you walk beneath them, a reverent hush falls over you. The soundless sound of awe. You are in the presence of venerable beings.

Near the entrance to the forest, there's a sign urging visitors to talk softly, turn off their cellphones, and keep kids under control. Farther along, in the heart of the forest where the tallest trees grow, a simple sign announces that you've arrived at a place called Cathedral Grove. And then, two words: "Enter Quietly."

Yes. Quiet. Noble Silence. Can we yield to its holiness? For the most part, at least on the day I was there, people seemed to be trying to honor that directive. But how sad that we even need to be cued.

This is not necessarily our fault. We live, most of our lives, in a bubbling soup of noise. Silence has become such a rare blessing that it's no surprise we've grown accustomed to the loss of it. Some of the symphony of sound surrounding us is neutral or even pleasant. But much of it is downright maddening.

For example: the aural horror of cryptocurrency computers. They run 24 hours a day, mining digital data, housed in massive warehouses, and they're cooled by huge industrial fans that emit a constant, low-level roar. The bitcoin companies operate largely under the radar and are nearly impossible to regulate. They tend to set up shop in rural areas where there are no noise ordinances. The unlucky people who live within a mile or two of these installations have been driven inside their homes by the incessant din. The sound also adversely affects wildlife, interrupting their patterns of reproduction and migration.

When I studied meditation in Burma, our teacher Michele McDonald told us something I wrote down in my journal. It was on a night when the village below our mountaintop monastery had erupted into a festival. Loudspeakers blared tinny music into the darkness, interrupted by sporadic cheers. Our peace was shattered.

As we gathered in the meditation hall for our evening sitting, frustration must have been evident on our faces. Michele looked at us with compassion. "The real noise in this world," she said, "is the reactive mind."

In other words, the problem was not the music. The problem was our aversion to the music, our inability to accept something being other than the way we preferred it to be. Michele recognized the mental commentary that was churning inside us. Left to its natural tendencies, the mind generates its own maddening noise. That's why, at various points during a silent hike, I stop the group. For a minute or two we stand silently in place, right there on the trail. I let them know at the beginning of the hike that whenever I halt our walk like that, they can use the short pause to re-collect their wandering mind. It's a chance to recognize that their brains were most likely filling the silence with inner chatter. As we stand there motionless, I hope my hikers are experiencing, if only for a moment, the rapture and relief of Noble Silence—both verbal and mental.

By the end of the hike, most groups don't want to leave the quiet. They come off the trail slowly, reluctantly.

"Does anyone want to share about your experience?" I ask. They usually just gaze at me, faces soft and eyes radiant. It's hard to speak again. Sometimes we simply stand in a circle and smile at each other.

I want my hikers to be able to take their experience of Noble Silence with them, back into the cacophonous world. As a benediction, I read them this teaching. It comes from a Taiwanese Dharma master named Hsin Tao:

Hear the silence in the mountains and rivers, the great wide earth, the sky. Eventually, the whole universe will fall into deep silence. Perceive that same deep silence in yourself.

Chapter 14

Kintsukuroi

A person who has survived trauma is like someone who just rode out a tornado in their basement. Once the wind subsides, they are stunned to find themselves in one piece. If they're able to move, they crawl out of the rubble, clawing their way upward.

Once they see sky, they stand. They're shaky … but they're alive, which feels like a miracle. They look around. Devastation everywhere. Utter stillness. No signs of life.

Am I the only one left? they think.

As adrenalin starts to surge, it becomes vitally important to look for other survivors. Surely someone else made it through the storm. They start tearing among the wreckage.

I've got to find others!

This is the premise of support groups. In the wake of tragedy, we need to connect with other people who've experienced something terrible, something similar to what we've been through. Somehow that bonding—even if it's with strangers—offsets the shock. It softens the sense of unreality.

In a support group, we listen to each other's stories. We bear witness to our shared traumas. Slowly, almost imperceptibly, we help each other heal. That's why individual therapy often is not enough. That's why I suggest to some of my patients that they try a support group.

The couple who lost a newborn I send to Compassionate Friends. The person coming to terms with a dysfunctional childhood I send to Adult Children of Alcoholics or Adult Survivors of Child Abuse. I know it will help for them to hear that all-important message: *You're not the only one.*

I, however, had no support group. There's no such thing as Monoculars Anonymous. And my search predated Facebook, with its wealth of online groups.

So I made my own support group, looking for other people who have lost an eye. Mostly it was online research, with the help of Google. Right away, it heartened me to find so many names of famous folks who are blind in one eye. I started a list. For each one, I noted whether they lost their right or left eye, at what age it happened, and how. There was something strangely comforting in the details of their stories.

Some were childhood accidents, like mine. Novelist Alice Walker lost the sight in her right eye at age 8 when her brother shot a BB gun in her direction. Jazz guitarist Ry Cooder stabbed himself in the eye with a knife when he was 4, while trying to fix a toy car. Harvard biologist E.O. Wilson reeled in a pinfish one summer day when he was a young boy, and one of the fish's sharp spines caught him in the eye. Sportscaster Dick Vitale blinded his left eye with a pencil in a kindergarten mishap.

Others lost an eye to glaucoma or other diseases (actors Rex Harrison, Sandy Duncan, and Peter Falk, rapper Fetty Wap). Some lost an eye in an accident during adulthood (Tibetan Buddhist scholar Robert Thurman, glass artist Dale Chihuly, Israeli general Moshe Dayan, boxer Michael Olajide Jr.).

Then there is British author Salman Rushdie, who lost his right eye in 2022 during a disturbing, caught-on-video attack. As Rushdie spoke to a large crowd at an open-air venue in New York state, a man rushed the stage and pounced on him with a knife. Rushdie survived the assault, but he now wears eyeglasses with the right lens blacked out. This spring, nearly two years after the attack, he released a memoir with a searing one-word title: *Knife.*

Reading all those names—knowing what functional lives those people lead, their contributions to the world in culture, literature, music, art, sports—was balm to my soul. I could easily imagine their struggles to overcome shame, their shrinking from others' judgments, the simple dread of being looked at. Despite it all, they triumphed. They did great things. If we were sitting together in a circle of chairs in a support group, I would cheer their successes.

Two of the names on my list of monoculars, James Thurber and Sammy Davis, Jr., had the same birthdate as mine, December 8. That revelation spooked me. It felt like some sort of strange karmic thread connecting us—people born on December eighth who lose an eye. On YouTube I found a clip of an old TV interview where Davis discusses the aftermath of losing his eye in a car accident. Every time I watch it, I tear up—not from sadness but from the solidarity of hearing a fellow monocular talk frankly about what it's like to live with this condition, the weird liminal space we occupy between normalcy and disability.

My research also turned up the disturbing stories of people who were shot in the eye while taking part in street protests. These people, most of them quite young, left home one day with two normal eyes and ended up maimed, half-blind. It has happened in various countries in recent years, including Iran, where thousands were protesting the death of a young woman while in custody for wearing her head scarf too loosely.

After the murder of George Floyd by a Minneapolis police officer in 2020, protests erupted in several cities in the United States—and eyes were lost to so-called "less lethal" methods fired by law enforcement into crowds of people. The police used bean bags filled with lead pellets, foam-nosed bullets, and pepper balls. A suspiciously high number of these projectiles hit people in the eye. The American Academy of Ophthalmology issued a statement condemning the use of these "less lethal" methods because of the spike in ocular traumas doctors were treating after each protest.

I've also heard sad stories from my ocularists. During the hours we sat together while they crafted a new prosthesis for me, they would tell me about some of their other patients. One man lost his eye to a rope that whipped through the driver's side window of his truck as he was trying to yank a stump out of the ground. Another person washed his face with city water that had somehow gotten infected with the infamous "brain-eating amoeba." It didn't eat his brain, but it destroyed his eye.

One ocularist told me that some of his patients were "botched suicides"—people who shot themselves in the head and survived, but suffered a devastating injury that blinded them in one eye. He also said at least 200 of his patients lost their eye to a BB. Like the young girl who was inside her home when someone shot a BB gun out in the yard. The BB ricocheted off a paper plate nailed to a tree, then blasted through the screen door and hit a glass lamp inside the house. The lamp shattered, and a shard of glass flew into the girl's eye. That sequence of events probably took all of three seconds.

An eye can be lost in the space of a breath.

Each story I heard or read, each famous name I unearthed, was a rung on a ladder, helping me climb out of the rubble. Slowly, subtly the needle moved away from shame, away from a sense of being defective. It's the all-important difference between *"something's wrong with you"* versus the much more compassionate *"something*

happened to you." Something happened to them too, these people I'll never meet but with whom I have a kinship. We're linked by our shared histories, our communal experience of living with only one eye.

Every therapist who treats survivors of trauma understands this concept. The therapy is all about unburdening from the shame. It's also about reversing the tendency to blame ourselves, as if we stupidly or arrogantly created the trauma that wounded us. Trauma therapy is hard work because sometimes self-blame and shame have been riding our backs for decades.

Andrew Vachss, an author and human rights attorney who wore an eye patch over his damaged right eye, did not like the term "survivors" for those who've experienced trauma. There's no heroism to living through trauma, he said. If we survive something terrible, if we somehow recover from the unimaginable, it's happenstance. Good genes. Sheer luck.

Vachss preferred the term "transcenders" because he was more interested in how people fare after the trauma is over. He said those of us who come out of trauma and manage to live a psychologically healthy, functional life are the people who've transcended trauma. Those are the people on my list of monoculars. That's my tribe.

Before the telehealth era, when I was still seeing psychotherapy patients in person, I kept a framed photo on a table in my office. It was near the loveseat where my patients sat, so it would catch their eye. The photo showed a lovely pottery bowl, threaded with jagged lines of lacquer that looked like lightning bolts. The bowl had been broken, then pieced back together by sealing the cracks with gold leaf. It's a Japanese art called *kintsukuroi.* The word means "to repair with gold."

The caption on the photo explained that *kintsukuroi* is a way of understanding how something—an earthen bowl, a human being—is more beautiful because it has those cracks.

It was broken. Now it's beautiful.

Most of my trauma patients eventually noticed that framed photo on the table in my office. I never pointed it out. They just seemed to gravitate to it naturally. We would pronounce the word together, slowly, until it felt comfortable in their mouths. Then we'd discuss the concept of turning brokenness into beauty. I let them make the connection to whatever their own cracks were, and how we were applying gold leaf to those cracks through the work we did together.

Many of my patients used their phones to snap a photo of the framed picture, so they could remember. One later decided to have the word *kintsukuroi* tattooed on her arm.

What they didn't know is that I am also a broken-and-repaired bowl. Just like them. We're all crawling upward, out of the rubble. Trying to be transcenders.

Chapter 15

Meeting Awareness

My friend Susan wanted to paint my portrait.

She was hesitant when she approached me with the idea because she knew how I cringe at cameras and mirrors. She understood that the thought of having my likeness on a 3-by-4-foot canvas—the eyes many times larger than real life—would make me squeamish.

But we've been friends for a long time, and I trusted her. Susan is a gifted artist. This portrait would be part of an ambitious project she had been developing for years, maybe the most important work of her career. I wanted to support her.

So, yes ... I agreed to pose for a portrait.

Susan and I met through meditation. More than a decade ago, we both ended up at a Unitarian-Universalist church that allowed us to borrow its sanctuary on Saturday mornings. We formed a meditation group, a few other folks wandered in, and thus began our partnership of shared spirituality. Twenty years separate Susan and me in age but we're kindred spirits, both of us introverted and more comfortable with solitude than socializing.

As I got to know Susan, I was blown away by the quality of her paintings. She studied at Cooper Union, the prestigious art school in New York City, then earned an MFA from Columbia University. She has had solo exhibitions at galleries in the United States and France. She moved to South Carolina when her husband got a job teaching philosophy at Clemson University. Later they moved back to Susan's home state of Alaska.

Susan's paintings are lush and colorful with a dreamy, diaphanous quality. She puts on the canvas what she sees in her mind's eye, which is the product of a far-ranging imagination. Her themes are existential and her images often allegorical, expressing what she calls "a sense of the transcendent."

Several years ago, Susan painted something more realistic than her usual subjects. It was an oversized portrait of one of our friends, a close-up of the woman's face. All of us who saw the painting were immediately struck by the subject's eyes. They drew you in and held your attention. They seemed to be telegraphing something important.

That was the beginning. Susan had found her calling. She became obsessed with painting faces, many times larger than life, and so detailed that photos of the finished paintings made them look like giant photographs. Her ability to capture the subtleties of skin tone, the faint shadows of facial muscles, the multilayered depth of human eyes was mesmerizing.

She spent months on each portrait, patiently applying layer upon layer of oil pigments, working from a photograph of her subject. I was fascinated by her process and how it grew into a spiritual exercise for her. She told me it was like meditation, her hours standing in front of the easel, being in the presence of the person on the canvas. Surprisingly, she wasn't trying to capture a perfect likeness of the person.

"Photo-realism is not my goal," she said. "I want to dive deeper into what it means to meet someone directly, to gaze into their eyes and feel that sense of timelessness, with no separation created by the mind."

That's one thing I love about Susan, that she comes out with beautiful sentences like this.

I asked her once how she knew when a painting was done, when she had achieved all she hoped for. "It feels like I'm tuning into a resonance or a radio signal," she said. "And I know I'm finished when the signal is finally clear."

Susan's studio when she lived in South Carolina was a small space carved out of one half of her garage. A bank of three windows provided natural light. Thin Oriental rugs warmed the cement floor. I was attracted to the glass jars filled with paintbrushes of all sizes and the palettes speckled with rainbow blobs of dried paint. The whole room was a Vermeer still-life.

As Susan finished the portraits, one by one, they joined a gallery of faces hanging on the particle-board walls. She started calling the series *Meeting Awareness,* which seemed to me the perfect title. You'd walk in the studio and huge eyes would peer at you from all sides of the room. You were meeting the awareness of each of those people in a direct face-to-face encounter. The experience stunned me into silence, every time.

Similar to when I was a teenager brooding over the beautiful eyes of models in fashion magazines, I gazed at those eyes in Susan's portraits, feeling a mix of envy and wonder. What must it feel like to have a pair of perfect eyes, to stare with such poise at the artist, to allow that person to look through your eyes into your soul and capture it on canvas?

When Susan's father was diagnosed with a terminal illness, she decided to include him in her collection of portraits. She took his photo at a time during the cancer treatments when he was feeling fairly well. In the photograph, his face looked pensive and a bit sad, with what Susan called a "sweet innocence" in his eyes. After his death, she poured her grief onto the canvas. During the long months she worked on that painting, Susan was quiet. She would appear at Saturday morning meditation and settle into the stillness as though it were a refuge. She told me later that painting her father's portrait was a deeply healing experience.

"I realized in essence who he was—that which cannot die," she said. "And in the end, I was left with only gratitude and love."

By the time Susan asked me to pose for a portrait, the *Meeting Awareness* collection included seven paintings. I would be number eight—and potentially, she said, the last. That felt like an honor. She told me her technique had advanced quite a bit over the nine years of this project, as she learned more and more how to portray the intricacies of a human face and the spirit that illuminated it. I, as her last subject, would be the lucky recipient of a gift in full flower.

How could I not say yes?

The process began with Susan taking some close-up photos of me. She wanted at least one shot that could serve as her model. When she pointed her camera at my face, I had to fight down the instinctual wince. I felt naked and exposed. I was 64 by then, but still struggling with my age-old echoes of shame.

How will my eye look? fretted the voice of trauma in my head. *Is this going to turn out like every other photo of me? Will my weird eye mess up Susan's collection of portraits? Wouldn't she rather paint someone with two normal eyes?*

The voice was shrill, and it wouldn't shut up.

I guess the inner turmoil showed on my face, because neither of us were pleased with that first round of photos. I wasn't sure if it was my eye that had caused the problem, and I was afraid to ask. Susan said she wasn't happy with the lighting, but that sharp-tongued voice in my head wouldn't quite let me believe her. We shelved the project for a few months.

Eventually, Susan invited me back to her house. We sat in her screened porch, a lovely space enveloped by trees. It was early morning, with soft, translucent sunlight. Birds were everywhere in the trees, belting out their greetings to the day.

This time, she didn't take the photographs right away. First, we sat for thirty minutes in meditation—her suggestion. We had done that together in this place many times before. I was comfortable, calm, at home. Susan and I have shared so much silence over the years; that is where we connect most deeply.

At the end of the half-hour, she came and sat opposite me with her camera, quite close. As we chatted in our meditation-softened voices, she snapped a few photos. It was easy, non-threatening, almost like an extension of the meditation period. We clicked through the images on her viewfinder.

"These will work," she said.

Over the next few months, Susan kept me updated on the portrait's progress. Whenever she mentioned it, I felt a nervous flutter. I was intensely curious to see it but didn't want to be pushy. Then one day she asked if I'd like to come take a peek. "It's only about halfway done," she said. "But I want you to see it."

When I stepped into her studio, I took a moment before turning to face myself, that enormous me on the opposite wall. Of course, my attention went first to the eyes. To my surprise, they looked completely normal. Is that how they were in the photo she took? I couldn't remember. Susan was waiting for a response.

"It's … amazing," I said. And it was.

She started explaining what she had done so far, and what areas of the canvas needed more work. I tried to listen, but I was transfixed by the eyes: two huge brown orbs staring solemnly at me. Then I noticed something: One pupil—the one in the right eye, my artificial eye—was slightly larger than the other one. I was relieved to see that. I didn't want perfection; that would have been a lie. Although the eyes looked almost identical, Susan had found a subtle way to portray the difference. I loved her for that.

"I think your transmission is starting to come through," she said, standing behind me. Her voice sounded shy.

I remembered Susan's artist's statement, her goal of evoking what she calls her subject's "awakeness." It isn't about whether an eye, or any other physical feature, is normal or perfect—whatever those words mean. It's about something much more profound in each person, something untouched by trauma or injury. Susan's portrait of me, even in its unfinished state, glimmered with that potential.

I turned and gave her a hug.

"Thank you so much" was all I could manage. Anything else would have been superfluous, and we both knew it.

Three months later, Susan announced she was finished. The invitation to view the final product came on a chilly day in early spring. This time, I wasn't so apprehensive. I had an idea what to expect.

The portrait still hung on the wall, exactly where it had been all these months while Susan worked on it. As I stood there and faced myself, this giant self, there was the same odd sense of knowingness I felt several months ago. I recognized the person in the painting, yet I didn't.

Is that me? Am I her? Is this what people see when they look at me?

She seemed so serene, this woman with her calm eyes and a whisper of a smile.

I told Susan it was masterful, that I loved it, that she had achieved something extraordinary. Tears welled in my eyes. At first I tried to hide them from her. Then I realized that was pointless. She deserved to see how moved I was.

I looked around the room at all the other portraits—those faces with their perfect eyes, rendered in exquisite detail by Susan's paintbrush. I thought about all the years of work that went into this collection. I thought about her mission to bring forth and portray the true self of her subjects, including me. And I realized, with a singing heart, that I had my place in this gallery of faces.

I have my place in this world.

Chapter 16

The Eye of God

That day, the sun would go dark in the sky. And I was there to see it, along with 50,000 other people. The date was August 21, 2017. Later that afternoon, a total solar eclipse would begin its high-speed journey across the United States, as the moon and Earth lined up perfectly so that the moon passed between us and our star, obscuring it from view. Traveling about 2,000 miles an hour, this celestial spectacle would cross the continental United States in just over an hour and a half, beginning in Oregon and ending in South Carolina, where I was.

Ancient people were terrified of these events. Without warning the sun disappeared from the sky, leading them to believe it was the end of the world. Shaking with fear, they looked up at a blackened sun with its encircling ring of white light, and called it "the eye of God."

Like a lot of people, I had never seen a total solar eclipse. They're not exactly rare, occurring two to five times each year, but with each one, only 0.5% of the Earth's surface is darkened by the moon's shadow. So we're hardly ever in the right place at the right time to see one. The 2017 total solar eclipse was the first one in a century that had been visible in so many parts of the United States.

By sheer luck, I lived in a place that was "ground zero" along the eclipse path, where we would enjoy one of the longest times of totality: 2 minutes and 37 seconds. It was also sheer luck that six months before that, my husband Jim took a job as communications director for the College of Science at Clemson University. When he heard about the eclipse that would cross directly over the university's campus in August, Jim immediately started campaigning for the College of Science to sponsor a huge event, a community eclipse-viewing party.

The university was no stranger to huge events. On fall Saturdays, more than 100,000 people crowd into the small town of Clemson to cheer the football team. Clemson Tiger fans are a plentiful and passionate bunch. On football Saturdays, a massive police presence is needed to handle the traffic bottlenecks. So Jim knew that Clemson could handle a big gathering on campus to view the eclipse. But who would pay for this event? And who would handle crowd control? And where on campus would the event be held?

It took a while, but he finally convinced Clemson's administration that this was a chance for the university to shine, that inviting the public to a massive, free eclipse party was once-in-a-century good publicity. Thanks to his enthusiasm, Jim became the lead coordinator for an event dubbed "Eclipse Over Clemson" on behalf of its official sponsor, the College of Science. For the next six months, he worked overtime with a crew of colleagues and an external marketing firm to plan the logistics: traffic control, parking, shuttle buses, security, media, concessions, volunteers, emergency medical personnel, tents, food trucks, entertainment, a stage.

A special Eclipse Over Clemson webpage was created, then updated countless times. Fifty thousand pairs of cardboard eclipse viewing glasses were ordered, along with thousands of cases of bottled water. Jim fielded media inquiries from the *New York Times, Washington Post, Wall Street Journal*, National Public Radio, NBC, ABC, Fox News, and the BBC. I didn't see him much during those six months. As August 21 approached, his workdays stretched longer and longer. At home, he obsessively checked weather forecasts for the big day. During the final countdown of the last week before Eclipse Day, his anxiety crested.

"What if it rains?!" he fretted. "What if a cloud covers the sun during totality?!"

There was no answer to those questions, of course. We just had to hope. We were at the mercy of the weather gods.

Now it was Eclipse Day and Jim had been on campus since before dawn. When I arrived about 9 o'clock, he already had greeted dozens of TV crews and helped them set up for the day's coverage. Their satellite trucks took up an entire parking lot. He was also overseeing a group of researchers from the University of Maine who planned to launch a high-altitude balloon that would take photos of the eclipse at 110,000 feet.

Jim waved to me across the rapidly growing crowd but didn't have time to linger.

I would rather have been at home, frankly, or maybe on a quiet hilltop with a few friends. My ideal scenario for viewing this eclipse would be something solemn, meditative, maybe even in silence. I'm never a fan of big crowds, especially for something that has the potential to be a spiritual experience. Instead, I had arrived at a circus along with thousands of boisterous people, all in the mood for a party. But this was Jim's big day, probably the biggest of his career, so I was here to support him.

As the sun climbed higher in the sky, the temperature rose into the low 90s. The sky was blessedly clear—so far. Music blared over loudspeakers, and a continuous stream of people flowed onto a grassy field in the center of campus, carrying broad-brimmed hats, umbrellas, and folding chairs. Volunteers circulated through the crowd, passing out free water, cardboard fans, and eclipse glasses.

By midday the excitement was rising, along with oven-like temperatures. The mood was ebullient. A giant beach ball was batted around the crowd. Someone sprinted across the grass wearing a full-body *Tyrannosaurus rex* costume. The Clemson Tiger marching band, 300-strong, arrived in their purple and orange uniforms and pumped out several high-energy songs. I didn't know how they were able to do it in that sweltering heat.

Just after 1 p.m. the first phase of the eclipse began, and a sense of urgency electrified the air. People started putting on their cardboard glasses. All day, the scientists and astronomers giving talks from the stage had reminded us that eye damage can happen if you forget to wear the glasses while looking directly at the sun during an eclipse.

"Be sure to wear your solar shades until totality starts," they told us, over and over. Every time I heard the announcement, I was happy. Now everyone was like me, thinking about their eyes and protecting them. We were all in this together, monoculars and binoculars alike.

At 1:07, the dark disk of the moon bumped against the rim of the sun. On the southeastern horizon, a few clouds were massing. I watched them nervously. Which way were they moving? Might they float in the wrong direction and ruin everything? Please, no! Off in the distance, I could see Jim being interviewed live on camera by a Weather Channel reporter. I imagined he was watching that cloud bank, as I was.

I looked around. Thousands of faces were now tilting toward the sky. It looked like a mass worship service in honor of the sun god. Excited murmurs rippled through the crowd.

"It's starting!" crowed Rick Brown into a microphone. "First contact!"

Brown, a jovial man with a headful of white curls, is a self-proclaimed "eclipse chaser," one of a fraternity of well-heeled people who have the resources to travel all over the world, wherever and whenever there's a total eclipse of the sun. These people are like the obsessed birders with their life lists. The eclipse chasers maintain records of how many countries they've visited in their pursuit of the experience. They keep running tallies of their cumulative "time in totality."

Brown saw his first total solar eclipse as a teenager in 1970. Since then, he has chased the high in 13 countries, including Brazil, Venezuela, Mexico, Antigua, Turkey, Indonesia, Australia, Thailand, China, and several countries in Africa. During the 1990s, he hosted eclipse tour groups. Brown's time in totality is a whopping 50 minutes.

"It's an indescribable, unearthly sight," he said. "It looks like a black hole opening up in the universe. It makes the hair on the back of your neck stand up. People cry."

After viewing fifteen total solar eclipses, Brown decided that Clemson, South Carolina would be the best place to see number 16. He had come from his Long Island home to provide running commentary for us newbies. He was the epitome of an eager guide, boyish in his enthusiasm.

As more and more of the sun disappeared behind the moon over the next hour, Brown prompted us at one point to look toward the western horizon. There was Venus, shining brightly—in the middle of the afternoon, when we normally never see it. I heard gasps in the crowd, and a few cheers.

2:08. The sun looked like something had taken a huge bite out of it. I noticed the air starting to cool. My daylong coating of sweat had dried. The clouds that were threatening to obscure the show moved slowly away from what was left of the sun, as if they were agreeing not to interfere. The sky was now completely clear—but no longer sunny.

An odd kind of light settled over us. It wasn't quite darkness and not exactly like shade, either. Just flat, and eerie. An indescribable shade of gray. Or green. Or navy blue. I wasn't sure. Is this what our world would be like without the sun? It was unnerving. There was also a bit of a breeze, like the ones that kick up at dusk.

2:35. The sun was mostly covered now. Everyone around me was on their feet, peering upward. Brown announced over the loudspeakers that it was almost time for the "diamond ring." Just before the sun disappears completely, one last sparkle of sunlight flares at the edge of the corona for a dazzling moment or two. It looks like a giant solitaire engagement ring. Even then, Brown warned, we should keep our solar shades on.

"After that, when what you're seeing goes completely black, give it another two or three seconds," he said. "Then it's safe to take them off."

Finally the moment we'd been waiting for arrived. It was 2:37. We were in totality. Everyone, including me, ripped off the cardboard glasses. The sun was no longer a blinding, burning orb in the sky. We could look at it, for those next two and a half minutes, with our naked eyes. When would we ever in our lives have this chance again?

Brown was silent. He knew from experience that words were insufficient at that point. He was letting us discover the miracle for ourselves.

As the light dimmed further, I could see stars sprinkled across the sky. Thousands of milky white cellphone screens rose above our heads, an army of blank eyes all peering at the sun.

For a second, that annoyed me. What is this compulsive urge to film everything we see? Can't people just experience wondrous things without recording it on their phones? Then, inexplicably, I didn't mind. Those little points of light were candles in the dark, our instruments of worship. They were the cigarette lighters held aloft at 1970s rock concerts, expressing what we have no words for.

We were the ancients, our mouths agape, hearts thumping, arms lifted to the sky in veneration.

Jim had found his way to my side. His labors were finally over, all the interviews done. His fervent hope for an amazing day, the experience he so wanted to provide for thousands of people was happening, here and now. We clasped hands.

For two minutes and 37 seconds, awe was palpable in the air. I heard people talking around us, but their voices were low, respectful. The atmosphere of sharing something life-changing, something profoundly ineffable, prickled my skin.

Above us, a black sun floated silently in the semi-darkness, ringed by its corona of white fire. Hushed and reverent, all 50,000 of us beheld the eye of God.

Then it dawned on me: I could see this eclipse as well as anyone else in the crowd. My experience was not different from or lesser than. I have only one functioning eye but right then, that didn't matter at all, as we lifted our faces in unison toward the glorious spectacle in the sky. I suspect all of us, one-eyed and two-eyed alike, were giving thanks for the miracle of sight, rejoicing in the great gift of being able to see such a thing as this.

I turned to Jim. His eyes were filled with tears. So were mine. Both my eyes.

Chapter 17

Search for the Truth

My relationship with honesty has been a bumpy ride.

I think most people who know me consider me to be a kind person, with an abundance of compassion and generosity. Over the years, I've also honed my ability to be patient. Thousands of hours sitting motionless on a meditation cushion will do that for a person. Its purifying fire burns all impatience out of you.

Honesty? Quite a different story. Developing that virtue has been more of a struggle for me. I don't remember telling a lie in my childhood. If I had, I would have gotten in big trouble. Telling the truth was a mandate I absorbed by osmosis. The message came from my parents, from Sunday school, from *Mister Rogers Neighborhood* and my learn-to-read library of Golden Books. Pinocchio was the warning beacon. If you lie, you'll grow a gargantuan nose.

At 17, I shoplifted once. That debut act of dishonesty happened in a Dallas department store. I was walking past the glittery cosmetic counters. As I neared the Elizabeth Arden display, I noticed a stack of small paper shopping bags lying on the counter. They were white with red plastic handles. The Elizabeth Arden logo was inscribed on each side, along with lovely art of red geraniums growing in a window box. It was a promotion for their new lipstick collection, "Window Box Colors." It appeared that if you bought some Elizabeth Arden makeup, you'd get a geranium bag. I could see the clerk standing with her back to me, dropping a customer's purchases into one of those cute little bags. Instant lust stirred in me. I wanted a geranium bag, and I wanted it bad. But I couldn't afford any Elizabeth Arden cosmetics.

I hesitated for a moment—no more than a couple of seconds—and then, as I glided past, I grabbed a bag off the top of the pile. Walking fast, I made my getaway. It was only a miniature paper bag, probably worth 2 or 3 cents, and my crime hadn't exactly caused a ripple in the fabric of the universe. But it was a turning point. I'd crossed the line between virtue and non-virtue.

In college, when I fell in love with someone who wasn't mine to love, I learned a new ethic. To maintain that relationship, to keep that man in my life, I had to lie. I lied to a lot of people—my parents, my friends and classmates, myself. I became damn good at lying, and also at ignoring the gnarled fingers of guilt that twitched inside me. In fact, the lie I was living became a refuge. It was a place where I could hide from the truth I didn't want to see.

Years later, after I became a Buddhist, I learned about *sila*. Pronounced SEE-luh, sila is a word from the ancient language of Pali. It's usually translated as "morality," but that word has a

Calvinistic heaviness to it. I prefer one of the other translations: "virtue" or "ethics." Sila, I came to know, is vitally important on the spiritual path. I could meditate incessantly and read every Buddhist text I laid hands on. But if my moral code was flimsy, if I wasn't working to cultivate sila, I'd never get anywhere. It's a foundational teaching of Buddhism that the practice of sila is equally as important as mental development. They go hand in hand as we walk the spiritual path.

Once, years ago, I confessed a wrong to my spiritual teacher, Bhante Gunaratana. It was so hard to tell him what I'd done. My voice was shaky. There's no such thing as "confession" in Buddhism, but it's good practice to be truthful and discuss a lapse with your teacher. Bhante listened to my story, his face a calm pool of equanimity. Then he quoted a verse from the Dhammapada, a classic Buddhist text. This verse is often used to illustrate the value of virtue.

Whosoever was heedless formerly
But later lives with heedfulness
Illuminates the world
As a moon freed from clouds.

A moon freed from clouds. Those words inspired me to embrace the practice of sila, and that caused a huge shift in me. I grew to love truth, and the clarity it brings. How it cleans the glass, makes everything bright and clear. I understood, finally, that truth is not a

Mount Everest we're trying to climb. It's an ally. It's our sherpa on that climb.

Eventually, learning the truth about what happened to me in our family's kitchen that afternoon in 1959 became more important than ever. I knew, of course, that somehow I'd been injured and lost the vision in one eye. I had lived with that truth my whole life. But I still didn't know for sure how it happened. Memories of the trauma were buried in a dark corner of my mind, and the mystery troubled my heart.

So I decided to go to the one person who would know the truth. The person who was with me that day.

＊＊＊＊＊＊＊＊＊＊＊

The first time I asked Mother for the truth, I had come from Florida for a visit. We took a drive into the mountains to see autumn leaves. When I brought up the subject of my eye injury, we were sitting in a tea house in the tourist town of Highlands, tucked into an English-style spread of scones and cucumber sandwiches. A pot of Earl Grey sat on the flowered tablecloth between us.

"Please don't ask me about that in public," Mother said.

I was alarmed to see tears welling in her eyes. I was 30 years old. The accident happened 28 years ago. Surely we could talk about it now.

No. We could not.

I went home to Florida and within a month, I was in a courtroom legally changing my first name to Jeanne. Dumping the name on my birth certificate, the "Norma Jean" I had shared with Mother my whole life. Even though I'd gone by the nickname "Jeanie" since high school, I now wanted something more official, something elegant. Becoming "Jeanne," with its French spelling, felt like a way to declare my distance from Mother, my frustration with the fact that she still wouldn't—or couldn't—give me the truth. A truth that should be mine.

She was unaware I'd written a letter to the hospital in Baltimore seeking my medical records. I'd also gotten in touch with the first physician who saw me all those years ago, the family doctor who came to our house and tried to examine my eye while I lay in my brothers' bunk bed. He was now retired, but he graciously answered my letter.

Your mother was overcome with grief that she did not prevent you getting injured, the doctor wrote to me. *I think that is why she won't discuss this with you.*

I understood that. I did. But I was on a hunt. A hunt for the truth.

The story I'd been told for decades didn't feel right. No one saw me injure the eye, my parents said. I came to my mother whining and rubbing the eye, they said. Was it a toothpick? A sharp toy? A pair of scissors? We're not sure, they said. We'll never know.

I couldn't accept *"we'll never know."* I needed surety, not theories.

There was a clue in the doctor's letter, a big one. Actually, it was much more than a clue. It was a door flung wide open. *As I recall,* he wrote, *you got into the kitchen and stuck a kitchen knife in your eye.*

I read that sentence over and over. The words blurred on the page. Had I found the truth at last? Was the doctor remembering it correctly? Is that why nobody would tell me what happened, why Mother wept at the mere mention of my accident?

I called my cousin Kathy. She's the oldest of us five cousins. She was 13 when my accident happened. She'd remember. Kathy confirmed what the doctor said. She recalled the tearful phone call from my mother to hers. A sister sharing her tragedy with her only sibling. "The baby" had an accident. It happened while Mother had her back turned, in our kitchen. She was peeling potatoes and she left the paring knife on the counter, within reach of little Norma Jean's highchair.

I wanted to reach through the phone and wrap my cousin in a hug. She had given me a monumental gift. Now I could exhale. I had the truth, at long last. I didn't tell Mother that I knew. I stored these new facts in a secret compartment of my heart. There was no need to talk to her about it. That would only reopen the wound.

The hospital never did cough up my medical records from 1959. I talked to someone in the records department who referred me to someone in archives who transferred me to someone in microfiche. As I was passed along the chain of command, I was led to believe this was possible, that I just needed to land with the right person. Finally an administrator e-mailed me and admitted they only keep records for ten years. They had nothing for me.

A decade passed. The summer before I turned 40, the *Times* sent me to England on a story assignment. I invited Mother to come with me. It was the year of her eightieth birthday and my fortieth. We both loved English gardens. It felt like time to make peace. We declared this our mutual celebration of landmark birthdays.

Somewhere on that trip—maybe as we were inhaling the heady scent of delphiniums at the Chelsea Flower Show, or maybe while we wandered the White Garden at Sissinghurst Castle—we found each other again. It felt good to let go of my old animosity, to be my mother's daughter once more.

A few years later, Dad died and Mother entered the painful land of widowhood. She was brave, but I knew she hated life without him. As her health started failing, we hired caregivers to be with her overnight. She called them her "babysitters." Ever independent, she balked at wearing the LifeLine necklace that would alert us if she fell. My brothers thought it was time to move her to a nursing home, but I dug in my heels. Mother wasn't a social butterfly; I knew she would be miserable without her privacy. As long as her long-term care insurance kept paying for the in-home caregivers, I wanted her to stay right where she was.

As my fiftieth birthday approached, Mother had entered her nineties. I didn't know how much longer she'd be with us. I thought about the lifelong wound between us. I wanted to unburden her of the guilt. I thought we both needed that.

The day I turned 50, I went to Mother's house in late morning. My whole life, we'd had a tradition of talking on my birthday at 11:14 a.m.—the time I was born. Either she called me, or I called her. Now it was hard for her to dial the phone and if I called her, she couldn't hear me very well. So on my birthday, I made sure I was at her house in person by 11:14.

She was sitting in her forest green leather chair in the sunroom. She looked fragile, her skin translucent and marbled with blue veins. Her long white hair was pulled back into the flat bun she called a "pug." That was the hairstyle she'd had her whole adult life—70 years.

I sat cross-legged on the floor next to her footstool. "Mother, I want a special birthday present from you this year," I started.

My heart was thumping. I wanted to do this carefully. She was looking at me with a question mark in her eyes. It didn't take much to overwhelm her anymore.

"Can we talk about the accident? Would you mind?"

She started crying immediately. I reached up and took her hand. "I want us to be able to talk about it." She nodded, still weeping.

Then we talked. For a long time.

When we'd said everything there was to say, I could see the relief in her face. I was relieved too. I wished we had done this years ago, but at least we'd done it now. The air in the room seemed lighter, almost effervescent. I stood and leaned down to give Mother a hug. She reached up from her sitting position. Her arms draped around my bowed neck. We pressed together awkwardly.

My best birthday, ever.

Years later, to my disappointment, I can't remember what we said to each other that day. I can't remember the crucial moment when she admitted she left the knife on the counter, too close to my highchair. I can't remember the moment I told her it's okay, that I'm okay, that she can let it go. Evidently my brain also wanted to let it go—hence the memory lapse. All I was left with was an emptied-out feeling of release. The heart's liberation from a lifelong burden.

Mother lived a surprising 10 more years. We threw a small party at home for her 100th birthday. It was my brothers John and Mark and me, plus her loyal caregivers. Jim took pictures and video. On the coffee table in the living room, I set up a display of photos of Mother's life, but she couldn't see them very well. She sat in her wheelchair and ate a sliver of chocolate cake. She was listless, very quiet. As if she were already leaving us.

Three months later, she died in her sleep in the wee hours of a Sunday morning.

I was at peace. Before she died, we had brought out the truth. We laid it on the table, and it was good for both of us. She released a burden she had carried for almost half a century, and I had the truth I'd been seeking all that time.

❧❧❧❧❧❧❧❧

But there was more truth. I found it several years later, when I finally opened a box of files I'd brought from her house to mine. In the file marked "EYE INJURY" was a cache of papers, everything she'd saved from our trip to Baltimore for my hospitalization and the months afterward. The file and its contents were sixty years old. I never knew it existed.

I sat down on the floor, took the file in my lap, and opened it. The hospital bills were there: $25 a day for a private room, $15 for anesthesia and operating room, $22 for drugs. The cancelled checks were there. The airline ticket stubs were there.

Numerous letters from my father to their health insurance company were also there. He kept carbon copies of each typewritten missive. He was frustrated by the insurance company's repeated requests for more information before they would pay on the claims. It also irked him that they refused to reimburse for travel expenses when my mother and I flew to Baltimore. After they paid only $75 of the $400 Johns Hopkins hospital bill, Dad wrote more letters of protest. Clearly he was handling the money side of things, while my mother looked after me.

The contents of the file also showed me how my parents cast about, searching for other doctors who might be able to help, even after the Johns Hopkins physician told them the vision in my injured eye was gone. I found scribbled notes with names of ophthalmic surgeons in New Orleans and Florida. The summer after my injury, they flew me to the University of Iowa Medical Center for a consult. Dad wrote to the insurance company asking for reimbursement for that trip too: *"We are still trying to save her sight."*

In 1963, four years after the accident, there was a return visit to Dr. Iliff, the ophthalmologist who oversaw my care at Johns Hopkins. He reaffirmed that my eye was permanently blinded. His recommendation: Get a scleral shell to cover it, but we should wait until I was a bit older and would be able to tolerate it.

All of that was news to me. Poring over that file folder was like reading the medical history of a stranger. I had no memory of any of it.

When I was 8, my parents tried for one last opinion. We made a visit to Birmingham to see a specialist in reconstructive eye surgery. He concurred that my best option was not surgery, but an artificial eye. Evidently, that's when my parents finally gave up hope that my eye could ever look or function normally. Later that year I received my first prosthesis.

As I sifted through the bulging file, I was happy to come across the doctors' notes. These were what I couldn't get from Johns Hopkins when I wrote to their medical records department. Here they were at last, typewritten on thinning onionskin paper. Mother saved our copies.

Then I noticed something. Both the local eye doctor I saw and Dr. Iliff at Johns Hopkins made nearly the same statement as they described their first encounter with me. "The patient was hit in the eye by an unknown object ... something which caused a corneal laceration."

I re-read those lines, not quite believing what was typed there. *An unknown object. Something...*

The realization washed over me, a bitter wave of salt: My parents lied to the medical professionals who were treating me.

When asked what happened, Mother and Dad gave the doctors the same vague story I grew up with, that they had no idea what pierced my eye—or where, or when. They made up a truth that wasn't true.

As I read the doctors' reports, my breath caught in my throat. I felt for a moment like I was suffocating.

Of course, it didn't really matter. I knew that. Even if the doctors had learned it was a knife that injured me, they would have chosen the same treatments. All they cared about was trying to save a severely damaged eye. Even so, I was stunned that my parents whitewashed the truth, presumably to absolve my mother of guilt. They couldn't bring themselves to tell the doctors she turned her back, left a knife on the counter, wasn't watching her toddler in the highchair.

Mother did tell the truth to the family doctor who made a house call in those first few frantic hours after my accident, the doctor who wrote me with his memories of that day. But by the time my parents took me to the next doctor, and the next, a cover story had been spun. They had created a sanitized version of the truth that would live on for decades.

I found another piece of crumbling paper in the EYE INJURY file. It was a letter from my grandmother to my parents. I hadn't seen Grandmother Libby's handwriting in years, but I recognized it right away. The date was February 4, 1959—a week after the accident. My grandparents lived in Oregon, thousands of miles from us, so news of my injury would have been slow to reach them.

Received your letter this morning, telling us about the baby, my grandmother wrote. *You don't know how sorry I am to hear this. She must be hurting so much—poor little thing. Do you suppose her eye was scratched by a fingernail? They cause infection very easy.*

Oh, my god. They lied to my grandparents too. They told them they didn't know how it happened. Another erasure of the truth. How did they think they could possibly withhold that from them? The shame must have been crippling. No wonder we all had to abide by the "don't know" story in the years that followed. Mother and Dad couldn't afford for the truth to spill out inadvertently. Even my brothers, who surely knew what happened, must have been sworn to secrecy—or at least silence. The lie had to be maintained, even if it meant I would never know my own truth.

Now, though, the truth had spilled out. All of it, told by these pieces of paper scattered on the floor around me like fallen leaves.

One after another, emotions surged in. Shock. Anger. Sadness. The only emotion I seemed to have enough energy to feel was sadness. I was sad for myself and my lost truth, for how incredibly long it took me to confirm the basic facts of a defining moment in my life. I was also sad for our family, for all of us—the frightened, guilt-ridden parents trying to thread their way through this tragedy, the brothers whose young lives were subsumed by what happened to their baby sister, the grandparents wondering if they'd ever hear the truth.

Then, surprisingly, wondrously, the sadness dissipated and I felt … gratitude. It poured in, as warm and sweet as honey, bringing with it tears. I felt so grateful that Mother saved all these things. She could have burned them or crumpled them into the trash. She could have destroyed all this evidence of the lie and put her sorrow behind her. But she didn't. She stowed these papers in a safe place, knowing that someday, probably after her death, I would read the contents of this file. She knew it would be important.

She wanted me to have the truth.

I slipped the papers into the file and put it back in the box where I found it. Even though I might never open the file again, I wasn't ready to let it go.

Some gifts are looked at only once—but cherished forever.

Epilogue

It's a midsummer Sunday morning. I'm in my kitchen making an omelet. Jim and I always share an omelet for Sunday brunch.

Outside the window, a sleepy-eyed sun crests Sharptop Mountain. Already the hummingbirds are dive-bombing our feeders on the back porch. We built this house in 2021, on a wooded parcel in the Blue Ridge Mountains that took me years to find. Hopefully this will be our last home. This is how, and where, we wanted to live out our retirement. It's a simple, peaceful life.

Today's omelet features fresh eggs we get from our neighbors at the community farm down in the valley. I also have a beefy heirloom tomato I'm going to slice, for a burst of color and flavor.

I open the knife drawer. I'm looking for my serrated knife, but my hand falls randomly onto something else, a smaller knife I don't use very often. I bring it out to take a look.

It's a paring knife. Exactly like the one my mother used for peeling potatoes when I was little. Exactly like the one that lay on the kitchen counter next to my highchair, the knife that altered the course of my life.

Standing here in my own kitchen, sixty-five years after that day, I look at the knife resting in my hand. Its blade is not long, about four inches. It doesn't look nearly as menacing as some of the other knives in the drawer, like my Japanese *nakiri*, with its big rectangular blade for chopping vegetables.

I imagine a 2-year-old holding this petite paring knife. Was she attracted to its shiny blade? Was she trying to see it more closely as she held it up to her face? Did she have any idea how it might hurt her?

I wonder, of course, what could possibly inspire that small child to plunge the knife into her eye. I think about the last moment before she did it, that moment when the karmic stream might have flowed in a different direction—but did not. Could not.

There's a famous sutta in which the Buddha talks to his disciples about dukkha, the great immensity of suffering in this world of samsara. He asks a rhetorical question about tears—all the tears we cry in our lives. Then he gives this summation:

"The stream of tears we have shed as we journey through this existence, through being united with the disagreeable and separated from the agreeable—those tears are more than the water in all the great oceans."

Dukkha can strike us at any moment. It pierces our eye of awareness with savage force. The Buddha understood this truth 2,568 years ago, living in a world so different from ours—and yet the same. The first of his Four Noble Truths is that dukkha pervades our lives. We've all experienced suffering in its myriad of forms. We have shed oceans of tears.

But there's also joy. There's the miracle that I have one functioning eye, this precious eye that has served me so well my whole life. With this one eye, I can see the face of my beloved. I can see the brilliant leaves of autumn, the million quivering shades of green in springtime. I can see the words on a screen as my fingers tap-dance across the keyboard, turning my thoughts into a piece of writing.

All these things teach my heart how to be glad, how to balance suffering with joy. This is not a platitude. This is what I know.

The Buddha warns us, though, that joy is evanescent. It's impermanent, like everything else. And the suffering returns if we cannot accept the truth of impermanence, if we don't allow joy to flow freely in and out, like the tide.

I know now. It's so clear to see. The action that blinded my eye was the ripening of karmic fruit. Nothing more, nothing less. It is done.

I put the knife back in the drawer. There's only one thought left in my mind.

I am safe.

Acknowledgements

My first bow of gratitude goes to **Jim Melvin,** the splendid human with whom I've shared the last 30-plus years. We met through the written word, in a third-floor newsroom, and it's been a wonderful ride ever since. Jim is the first person to read anything I write, and I am his first reader, even though our preferred genres are worlds apart. I couldn't do this life without you, my dear, and wouldn't want to.

I have been blessed with a small but sweet family: **John, Lia, Beth, Jill, Fred, Jaxson, Ella, Robin, Bob, Kerri, Daniel, Kathleen, Patty, Ashley, Kathy, Ellen, Maya, Metta.** And in loving memory: my brother **Mark,** sister-in-law **Sheila,** and nephew **Jeff.**

I owe abiding gratitude and much metta (lovingkindness) to my beloved spiritual teacher, **Venerable Henepola Gunaratana Mahathera**. Dear Bhante G, may you continue in good health to the end of your long life. May your wisdom and compassion ripple outward to all corners of the world, to benefit all beings.

I'd also like to thank the many other Buddhist teachers who have shared the richness of the Dhamma with me over the years, both in person and online: **Ayya Sudhamma, Bhante Dhammawansha, Bhante Rahula, Bhante Saddhajeewa, Bhante**

Wipulasara, Joseph Goldstein, Khenpo Konchog Gyaltsen, Jack Kornfield, Michele McDonald, Mark Nunberg, Sujata. And in memoriam: **Dae Soen Sa Nim, Roshi Peter Muryo Matthiessen, Ruth Denison, Sayadaw U Lakkhana, Venerable Dharmawara, Venerable U Silananda**.

Extra-special love goes to the wise and loving therapist who helped me dig out of my own emotional holes and later inspired me to follow in her footsteps: the beautiful soul who is **Caroline Fenderson**.

Then there are the beloved long-time friends, many of them in Florida, who've enriched my life in countless ways: **Linda Bias, Diana Grove, Margo Hammond, Carrie Kent, Gretchen Letterman, Diane Mason, Ann Schoenacher.** And in memoriam: **Erin James, Nancy Paradis.** Blessings to you all, my spirit sisters.

A special shout-out goes to **Janisse Ray,** a gifted wordsmith who cares deeply about the natural world and the written word. Janisse, you inspire me by who you are and what you do. Thank you for your unflagging support, your generous spirit, and how you shepherd all of us in the writing community.

I also want to send heartfelt thanks to the small army of readers and subscribers who helped me launch *Good Eye, Bad Eye.* Throughout the four months of this book's online serialization (June-September 2024), they showed up weekly to read each new chapter and share their thoughts and reactions. You all were champs and I thank you for being a part of that grand literary experiment.

As I mentioned in Chapter 9, all the ocularists who created eyes for me since my childhood hold a tender place in my heart ... but I'd especially like to acknowledge **Randy Minor** and **Emma Boyd.** You folks are wizards, and I love your magic.

Big thanks to my **Silent Hikers,** an intrepid bunch who've been with me for more than a decade, and also to the cherished friends with whom I've practiced meditation over the years: **Joanna Grabel, Yi Liu, Sriyani Rajapakse,** and **Susan Watson**. Sangha is such a blessing.

A tip of the hat to my colleagues in our therapy consultation group: **Ruth Harbin, Paulette Herbert, Eunice Lehmacher, Ashley Lester,** and **Cheryl Smart.** Also to those mental health clinicians who mentored me early on in my counseling career: **Margaret Axson, Tamara Houston, Carrie Pettit, Raquel Contreras, Birma Gainor, Lyn Stribling,** and **Elaine Hiott**. I wouldn't be the therapist I am without the inspiration I glean from all of you wonderful women.

Profound thanks go to two uber-talented people who were instrumental in helping me create the multimedia package for this book when it was serialized online: **BJ Callahan** of FNKY Music Studios and **Seth Williams** of Fiddle Head Media House.

I mustn't forget to thank the natural world, with her multitude of beings and her astounding, everlasting beauty. I find such solace in her company, and I am so grateful. This Earth is imperiled, at our own hands, and yet she carries on with grace. I find that so inspiring, even as it pains my heart.

And finally … a deep bow of thanks and love for my late father and mother, **Conrad and Norma**. After living through the upheavals of the Great Depression and World War II, they were determined their children would know stability and security. I was blessed in so many ways to be their daughter, to grow up never doubting that I was loved.

May all beings be well.
May all beings be safe.
May all beings know peace of mind and heart.

About the Author

Jeanne Malmgren was born in South Carolina and lived many places in the U.S. before returning home to the Blue Ridge Mountains in midlife. She is a wife, sister, aunt, mother, stepmother and grandmother. From an early age, she has carried on an ardent love affair with Mother Earth.

Jeanne holds two degrees from Clemson University: a B.A. in Spanish and an M.Ed. in clinical mental health. During her first career of journalism, she worked as an Associate Editor at *The Mother Earth News* magazine, then spent 20 years as a feature writer and editor at Florida's largest newspaper, the *Tampa Bay Times*. Her work there won awards from the Florida Society of News Editors, Society of Professional Journalists, and the American Association of Sunday and Feature Editors.

A longtime Buddhist and co-founder of a meditation center in Florida, Jeanne co-authored *Journey to Mindfulness* (Wisdom Publications, 2017), the autobiography of her spiritual teacher, the eminent meditation master Venerable H. Gunaratana. Some of her talks and guided meditations can be found on her YouTube channel.

In her mid-fifties, Jeanne launched a second career: psychotherapy. After working as a hospice grief counselor and with survivors of domestic violence, she founded a private practice of counseling, where she specializes in mindfulness- and nature-based treatment.

In recent years, Jeanne returned to her first love of writing. Her essays and articles have appeared in literary magazines, her popular online newsletter *Rx Nature* and in an anthology of nature writing, *Outdoor Adventures in the Upcountry* (Hub City Press, 2010). She was nominated for a Pushcart Prize and won a "Room of One's Own" writing residency from the Emrys Foundation for the Arts in Greenville, S.C. She's now bravely (or recklessly) trying her hand at fiction, diving into work on a historical novel set in the wild, mountainous corner of South Carolina where her heart lives.

A message from the author

Thank you so much, dear reader, for coming along with me on this journey through *Good Eye, Bad Eye*. My deep wish is that this book will offer healing and hope. Whatever traumas you or someone you care for may be carrying, I wish you a lighter load—in mind and heart. If you enjoyed reading my memoir, please let the world know about it by posting an online review. Any good words are very much appreciated.